# HUNTING DOG KNOW-HOW

# HUNTING DOG
# KNOW-HOW

*by*

DAVID MICHAEL DUFFEY

**REVISED EDITION**

———————

WINCHESTER PRESS

This edition is affectionately and respectfully dedicated
TO FLIRT
the little bitch who, along with many other gun dogs, played
an important role in the education of a dog trainer. Their
ability, effort and devotion made it fun and a privilege
to mold their destinies and revel in the results, the enjoyment
of a great outdoor sport at its highest level.

# Contents

# Acknowledgment

The author wishes to thank the editors of *Outdoor Life* for permission to reproduce the following photographs, which originally appeared in the pages of this magazine: Pages 2, 6, 11, 20, 27, 33, 34, 42, 52, 80, 99, 113, 116, 119, 138, 142, 151, and 162.

# HUNTING DOG KNOW-HOW

# 1

## *Why This Book Was Written*

A comparison of people with dogs may make some hackles rise on both sides, but since man and dog have now shared the ups and downs of life for untold centuries, perhaps comparison is inevitable.

After these centuries of association with humans, it seems that dogs have learned to understand us better than we've learned to understand them. At any rate, the dog's adaptibility to different situations and different people is a major reason for continued canine popularity, while man often fails to recognize that each dog, like each person, is both a unique individual and a possessor of certain generic traits. Just as there are varying racial characteristics among humans, so are there different breed characteristics among dogs.

Sportsmen who are long on enthusiasm but too short on know-how are often disappointed in their dogs; either they fail to obtain any training success, or they wonder why they are successful with some dogs, but fail miserably with others. Unfortunately, not every man can train a dog; nor can any man train every dog he encounters. We

1

can put it this way (and watch some parents' hackles rise): there are parents who can read up on child psychology till they've got eyestrain, but who'll still have trouble coping with their kids. It's the same thing in the dog game.

Thus a book like this can only be an aid. Training a dog takes more than reading about how to do it; it also takes the time and effort of actual practice. Only as a *doer* will you discover if you have a knack for dog training. But I hope that this book will make your training an enjoyable experience, rather than a puzzling, onerous chore.

The author believes in using the dog that's best suited to the job at hand. Here he is with five of his own dogs: German Wirehaired Pointer, English Springer, Chesapeake, American Water Spaniel and Labrador.

Because we can generalize about breed characteristics, it is possible to say that this or that breed usually responds to this or that method. As a result, many useful books have been written which deal with one group or one breed of dog. Some specialty books may tell a man how to train retrievers, for example, while others will detail procedures for training pointing dogs. But they are next to useless to the man who acquires a new dog which happens to be of a different breed than the one he owned when he bought the training book.

A man who successfully trains a retriever with the aid of a good book will draw a blank if he treats a pointing dog in the same manner. A man who does not know in advance what to expect of a certain breed in the field will wind up with a confused and worthless dog, and a wrongly prejudiced opinion about the breed.

Misunderstandings about the purpose in life of the various breeds are evident every day in the mail I receive and answer as part of my job as Dog Editor of OUTDOOR LIFE magazine. Readers ask why their Labradors won't point; why their English Setters don't fetch; why their Cocker Spaniels don't bring rabbits around like their Beagles used to. This may sound funny to the experienced dog man. But it is no laughing matter. The average sportsman has a very meager understanding of dogs and their place in the hunting scene. Lacking this knowledge, he cannot properly utilize even the best of the tried-and-true training methods.

Since there are three broad classifications of dogs used in "bird hunting" (which for our purposes includes upland and shore birds, along with waterfowl) there is a need for one book that will tell the "do-it-yourself" dog trainer not only what he has to know about the mechanics of training dogs of a number of different breeds, but *why* the training is done as it is.

The three "bird-dog" groupings—spaniels, retrievers and pointers—include our most popular hunting breeds. Today's sportsman needs some frank information as to what each breed is good for, and why some breeds are unsuitable for certain kinds of hunting. Too often the only source a sportsman interested in buying and training a dog has access to is the parent organization of a breed which refuses to recognize that there are some things a "rival" breed can do better.

So to achieve its purpose, this will have to be a controversial book. Based on the author's personal experience, it will point out what dogs are best suited for certain types of work, and attempt to give the would-be dog owner a line on what breed will be best suited to his temperament and way of doing things. While most dogs adjust to humans, many humans cannot adjust to dogs. You will do a better job of training your dog if you understand not only the hows and whys of training, but also recognize the fact that some breeds and some individuals are going to mesh well with your personality, while others will rub you the wrong way. This may require a bit of self-analysis on your part. So be honest.

This is not a book written by or for experts. Experts sometimes have the disconcerting habit of knowing all and learning nothing. This is a book for the hunter and the practical dog man—a man who not only knows that a good dog as a hunting companion will put more meat on the table, but who also gets a sheer enjoyment from good dog work which enhances his days in the field and can be savored in the long hours before the fire.

The opinions expressed in this effort to guide you in your selection and training of a bird-hunting dog are personal. But rest assured that they are also the result of many well and too many misspent hours of actual living and working with dogs. This is not just a re-written treatise on training dogs.

However, to deny the influence of professional trainers, interested amateurs and outstanding authorities in the field of dog training would approach the conceit of the self-made man who asserts that he did it all himself. I am deeply indebted to others who have stimulated and taught me much about dogs through their discussions and writings.

So, while few of the following training procedures are completely original (dogs and dog trainers, like humor and comedians, have been around for a long time)—and many of the opinions are strictly personal —at least whatever is recommended in this book has been tried with a dog or dogs. If it didn't work, I wouldn't suggest it.

# 2

## What to Expect
## from the Hunting Dog

It's ironic that in an age of specialization, most hunters seem to want a "jack of all trades." Because most bird hunters dabble in a bit of everything, giving whatever they run across a try, the dog of their desires is something they call an "all-round dog."

Actually, no such animal exists. For there can be no clear-cut definition of an "all-round" or "all-purpose" dog. But there are *multi*-purpose dogs. With proper training and enough experience, any of the dog breeds used in bird hunting can be expected to turn in a performance on more than one species of game bird.

It can be argued that to get the fullest enjoyment out of hunting with a dog a man should have a specialist for whatever particular game it is he seeks. As a practical matter, however, few of today's outdoorsmen have the time, money or facilities to support a string of dogs proficient in each aspect of the sport. It's one dog at a time.

So I know you're looking for a dog that will "do it all." But before undertaking to acquire and to train a dog that will handle more than

5

one species of game in an acceptable manner, the would-be dog owner must understand the specialty work for which each group of dogs—retrievers, spaniels and pointers—was intended. Only then can you understand the necessary modifications in training procedures which will serve to make an "all-round huntin' dog" out of a specialist.

Call this the revelation of a secret if you will. But don't ever forget it. To easily and successfully train a hunting dog, the trainer must first understand what the dog's instincts incline him to do, and then utilize this natural bent by channeling it into the work the trainer wants done.

A dog can be "broke" to do what does *not* come naturally. Sometimes this has to be done. But it's nice to know whether you're going to be toiling up an incline and battering your head against a stone wall, or if it's a downhill pull all the way.

For an opener, let's list the breeds included in the three general classifications of dogs best suited for bird hunting. This introductory handshake should help you understand what we're talking about when the breed names start to get flung about later in the book.

Under RETRIEVERS you'll find Labrador Retrievers, Golden Retrievers, Chesapeake Bay Retrievers, Curly-Coated Retrievers, Flat-Coated Retrievers and Irish Water Spaniels. As far as the Curly-Coats and Flat-Coats are concerned, you need only know that they exist. There

Good retrieves "put the frosting on the cake" for a day's shooting, and cut game wastage, too.

are a few in this country, but it's unlikely that you'll ever see one, much less acquire one. If you *want* a rare and different breed, they can be capable dogs. But whether through lack of promotion or failure to adapt to the ways and means of U. S. hunters, they just haven't caught on. The Irish Water is no longer a common dog either, but is well enough known for his capabilities to be assessed, and he might be acquired as a hunter.

In the SPANIEL classification the breeds include English Springer Spaniels, English Cocker Spaniels, Cocker Spaniels, American Water Spaniels, and four almost nonexistent breeds (Clumber, Field, Sussex and Welsh Springer Spaniels), with which a hunter needn't clutter his mind or vocabulary. Another spaniel, the Brittany, is included in the pointing dog category below, and the Irish Water Spaniel has been mentioned with the retrievers in that category.

The third, and most involved category, is POINTING DOGS. Two distinct types of pointing dogs are involved, and although they are asked to do essentially the same things in the field, their way of doing it has differentiated the more recently introduced "German" or "Continental" pointing breeds from the longer-established pointing breeds.

The Pointers (often called "English Pointers" to avoid confusion with the Continental breeds) and English Setters have the longest and most distinguished history in this country. Irish Setters and Gordon Setters are probably most properly grouped with the Pointer and English Setter, but for years they have attracted little attention from sportsmen who hunt and field-trial their dogs.

In the past quarter century, a "new" kind of dog that points its game has sky-rocketed in popularity among U. S. hunters. These are the breeds often referred to as "German," "European," "Continental" or "Multi-purpose" pointing dogs.

They have been highly touted, often to their detriment, as "all-purpose" dogs in contrast to the "specialist" Pointers and Setters. These dogs are pointers, for they do point their game. But they deserve the special treatment we'll accord them in this book, since despite their great popularity, very little has been written about them, specifically, to help fanciers of this type of dog understand and train them.

Breeds in this category are the German Shorthaired Pointer, the German Wirehaired Pointer, the Weimaraner, the Wirehaired Pointing Griffon, the Vizsla, and the Brittany Spaniel. All have docked (shortened) tails, in contrast to the "long-tailed" pointers and setters that originated in the British Isles. The Brittany and Griffon were developed in France, the Vizsla in Hungary and the others in Germany.

Let it be understood that ability and style are going to vary, not only between breeds, but to some extent among individuals belonging to the same breed. However, the general way each group may be expected to work, if used as intended, is listed below.

## RETRIEVERS

Their job is to walk, stand or sit quietly at a hunter's side, with their work taking place after the shooting is over. They mark and remember the places where shot birds dropped and, upon command, fetch these downed birds promptly, or diligently track down cripples in marsh,

The retriever's primary job comes after the game is shot. Until ordered to fetch, he walks quietly at the hunter's side, as this Labrador is doing.

open water or on dry land. Intended as waterfowl specialists, they have the physical and mental qualities to withstand the most arduous weather conditions, and to accept long periods of inactivity docilely.

## SPANIELS

Their job is to work busily in front of the gun, seeking out and flushing (putting into flight) upland birds from dense cover, yet staying within gun range and retrieving the birds knocked down. They are flushers, in contrast to the bird dogs who find and point game well out of gun range and "hold it" until the hunter's arrival. When retrievers are allowed to work before the gun, instead of serving solely as recoverers of shot game, they also work as flushers. An occasional "odd-ball" retriever or spaniel will point. This is frowned upon.

## POINTING DOGS

The work of dogs in this classification, being complicated by the different pace and style of the European breeds, incites more disagreement over what constitutes "good dog work" than any other category. The one thing these breeds have in common is their instinct—which must be carefully encouraged and nurtured—to point game and hold

Springer Spaniels can be expected to retrieve shot birds from land or water, and their willingness to work "the wet stuff" comes in handy when a pheasant falls in it, as this one did.

stanch until the hunter comes up and kicks out the birds. ("Stanch" or "staunch" in reference to a pointing dog means that he will point and hold his point until the handler flushes the birds. It is not to be confused with *steadiness*, which refers to a dog's actions *after* the birds are flushed. A "steady" dog holds his pointing posture after birds are flushed and shots fired, moving out again only on command. *Many pointing dogs flush their game.* This is highly undesirable. But in certain instances, hunters accept it, as a practical matter. This will be discussed in a later chapter.)

Pointing dogs, because they are supposed to "hold" birds once they've found them, are encouraged to hunt well out beyond gun range, covering a great deal of ground, and working body scent with a high head. A pointing dog that messes around too much with foot scent (pottering) is undesirable. But spaniels and retrievers, used as flushers, work with both foot and body scent. Pointing dogs may or may not be asked to retrieve. Many are taught to "point dead," thereby indicating to the hunter just where the downed bird is, although not actually picking it up and delivering it, as every spaniel or retriever is expected to do. To assure recovery of the downed bird is the important thing.

The conclusion you are safe in drawing from this general outline is that the spaniels, by natural bent and common usage, come closest

Retrieving is not the Pointer's strong suit, but they can be taught by using a feathered retrieving dummy, as Dave Duffey's Pointer demonstrates here.

to the dog that can "do it all." Their job is to find, flush and fetch any game in any cover the hunter may frequent. As might be expected, some retrievers will lack the initiative and ability to seek out and flush game, and many pointers will be failures in the retrieving department, particularly if the hunter insists on a soft-mouthed, snappy delivery of an unmarred bird.

Irish Setters are not primarily retrievers, but they can be taught to do the job well, as this one demonstrates by bringing in a pheasant.

Seldom can you expect your dog, if asked to do something outside his specialty, to do it in the outstanding manner of the specialist. But virtually all hunting breeds, we can safely say, can be called upon and trained to do a job outside their specialties, at least to the satisfaction of their individual hunter-trainers.

Some breeds, and of course, some individuals, adapt more easily than others. Which dogs can do *what* will be detailed in succeeding chapters as we discuss the personalities and physical capabilities of each breed mentioned, and the training approaches designed to get the most from each breed's natural bent and potential.

# 3

## Specific Breeds
## and Their Characteristics

No one is happy with mismatched socks or an uncongenial co-worker. So it is with men and dogs. While a talented trainer can teach a dog to do amazing things, thanks to the dog's eagerness to please and willingness to accept a pat on the shoulder and a kind word as rewards, much time and effort can be saved if a dog trainer realizes that some dog breeds are better cut out than others for certain jobs, and that some breed personalities won't mesh as well with the trainer's characteristics as others will.

Some people like dogs who fawn over them. Others prize independence. A man who can laugh at himself will accept some antics on the part of a dog that would enrage another. Getting the proper breed to start with is very important. Unless there is rapport and understanding between man and dog, no matter how good the intentions or how outstanding the abilities, a real training job will not be done.

Furthermore, where one man wants to hunt ducks, another prefers quail. The preceeding chapter has given you a line on breeds available for both specialty and all-round work. This chapter will be more specific. You don't have to accept my evaluations as "gospel." Maybe I just saw the wrong dogs. But give them some consideration. They're intended to help you in the proper selection of a dog, not to promote or knock any certain breed.

Trying to match your personality and hunting habits with a specific breed of dog may take a little self-analysis on your part. Come up with the right answers and it will help you appreciate and understand a dog you already have.

There's been a lot said about dogs reflecting their masters' personalities. Everyone from Fifth Avenue head-shrinkers to country horse doctors has had a crack at it. The consensus follows one of two theories. A man either picks a dog that strongly resembles him in character (and maybe even appearance), or else he picks a dog that is the antithesis of what he really is, but which represents what he would like to be. In other words, Milquetoast gets either a shy, retiring dog with which he can identify, or acquires some surly, obnoxious beast that lets him live out his secret desires through his dog.

That's all too deep for me. But I will offer my own theory, which I wouldn't want you to make a federal case out of either. You can bet that most of the dogs within any breed will reflect to a great extent what we've come to recognize as the characteristics and traits of the nationality or ethnic group of the country in which they were developed and became popular.

The "typical" German, or Irish, or English human personalities could not all be expected to be happy with the same type of response from a dog, it seems reasonable to conclude. But most of today's gun dogs were established and developed in the British Isles or Germany.

Thus as a result of natural selection and finally through specific choice, dogs with the personalities that pleased the human group they lived with became popular and were established as distinct breeds— which still transmit these personality traits to their off-spring, just as surely as they pass on their physical conformation.

All dogs do not conform to breed characteristics, nor do all persons from a specific ethnic group match the general pattern. There are dour Irishmen and non-militant Germans.

But it's a good bet that a man with a sense of humor, who won't crowd and push and will trade a "down in the dumps" act on one day for a superlative performance the next, will get along pretty well with a gun dog of Irish origin. Similarly, a man with an orderly mind, who demands perfection and is willing to impose the discipline and devote the time necessary to attaining it, will get the best response from one of the German breeds. The sincere, law-abiding good citizen, lacking the luster of more unstable compatriots, will find one of the English breeds his personal dish of tea.

But enough of that. There are all kinds of dogs for a man to choose from, and likes and dislikes are fortunate, for as the old Indian said, "Everybody think like me, everybody want my squaw."

In this chapter you'll find general descriptions of each breed of hunting dog. If you're interested in every last detail, you should consult the official standards established by the breed clubs and the American Kennel Club. You can study these breed standards, only glance at them or ignore them, as you prefer. You'll find that many good field dogs hardly resemble what the standard describes, and unless you have a background of equine and canine experience, you aren't going to understand half the terms used anyway. Why don't I explain 'em to you? It would take a book in itself to do it, and the pictures used here should speak louder than a spate of words. Finally, and frankly, I must confess that I'm not clear on a lot of the detail myself. Between you and me, I suspect that many of the learned *cognoscenti* who rattle on about "great propelling leverage," "elbows well let down" and so on, may have excellent memories but are no more "hep" to the practical application of the phrases than you or I.

Some persons have an eye for animals, just as others have a "green thumb." It's familiarity with working requirements and experience, along with this instinct, which tell a man who's sizing up an animal what type of performance this animal is likely to give, rather than memorization of a jargon attempting to describe what he can see.

Some are never able to recognize good physical conformation in dog, horse, man or woman. Others just don't care. So if you've picked a wife whose conformation lends itself to hoeing potatoes better than pirouetting on a dance floor, or your dog turns out to be a kind of petunia in an onion patch, don't let it upset you.

The proof of the puddin' is in the eatin'. A lot of "body beautifuls" have made no headlines in the athletic world while a lot of pot-bellied shortstops and flat-footed halfbacks have. By the same token, there are a lot of fine-performing field dogs who'd be turned away at the door of any benched show.

Desire, heart, guts—whatever you choose to call it—plus good basic instincts and sound training serve to overcome minor physical flaws, and the set of a dog's ear or the texture of his coat is less important than a trainable temperament and the kind of work his breed has proven it can perform satisfactorily. So my views aren't infallible. Dogs are individuals, and as a human I have my own enthusiasms and prejudices. But they will get you off on the right foot.

Some breeds which are very rarely seen in the field have been rather summarily ignored in this book. So you won't read much about the Wirehaired Pointing Griffon, Curly-Coated Retriever, Flat-Coated Retriever, Clumber Spaniel, Field Spaniel, Sussex Spaniel and Welsh Springer Spaniel. If you want me to be really honest with you, these esoteric breeds might be okay if you want to dabble in something virtually unique, but the fact of the matter is that I probably don't know much more about them than you do. So please pardon the omission.

## POINTER

The man who would like to hunt quail and prairie grouse and/or run his dog in pointing-dog field trials wants a Pointer. The breed can also be effectively utilized on all other upland game, such as pheasant, ruffed grouse, woodcock, chukar and Hungarian partridge. The best of this breed are virtual hunting machines.

Short-coated and easy-moving, the Pointer's forte is covering ground,

There's pride in every inch of him as this Pointer shows us what it means to "lock up high on both ends."

and instinct dictates that he reach out. They can be sensitive and pig-headed at the same time, and often show little concern for the where-abouts of the handler. This is not criticism. It's so you'll know what to expect. A dog ranging as far as a good covey dog does *must* be inde-pendent. If you know hounds and horses you'll get along well with a Pointer. If your experience has been with spaniels or retrievers, you'll have to do some adjusting.

If you admire style and dash, if most of your hunting is in "big country" with broken cover where the dog can be kept track of, and particularly if you hunt on horseback, the Pointer is your dog. He is not a good choice for restricted solid block coverts, and don't expect him to fetch ducks. In fact, if you want your upland birds retrieved, chances are good you'll have to force-train to get consistent results.

The Pointer is a specialist, pure and simple. He's at his best on quail, sharptail, prairie chicken and Hun in plantation and prairie country, and can be most satisfactory on pheasant, woodcock and ruffed grouse. He adapts well to kennel life, but is not generally kept as a companion dog; and he needs plenty of actual field work and ex-perience on birds to get and stay sharp.

## GERMAN SHORTHAIRED POINTER

Members of this breed make eminently practical gun dogs. They'll appeal to the man who walks heavy cover for pheasant, ruffed grouse and woodcock, who wants what he shoots picked up and brought back, but who also wants to shoot over a dog's point. Most Shorthairs lack the range, style and dash that a pleasing quail or chicken dog should display, although they can be used on those birds.

Shorthairs can be dealt with firmly. They respond to a lot of work and a "no nonsense" attitude, and can adapt to both kennel and house. If conditions are not too severe they can be used for jump shooting and retrieving waterfowl. Most take to water readily if properly in-troduced, and have good retrieving as well as pointing instinct; if not, they must be force-trained. German Shorthairs are required to retrieve as well as find and point game in field trials. Most pointer and setter trials don't ask for this, but most hunters desire it.

The Shorthair is the most popular of the so-called utility or Con-tinental pointing breeds, particularly favored by Midwest and West Coast hunters. A hardy breed that has proved itself, and while sometimes stubborn, is seldom prone to hurt feelings when corrected firmly, the German Shorthaired Pointer is a fine choice as a practical shooting dog for the man who isn't comfortable in the field unless he can keep track of his dog at all times.

German Shorthaired Pointers have been refined from the rather heavy, plodding dogs introduced in the U.S. in the late 1930's to more racy, wider-going field trial competitors like this one, owned by Ray Bauspies of Gurnee, Illinois.

## GERMAN WIREHAIRED POINTER

A relatively new breed in this country (recognized by AKC in 1959), the work the German Wirehair is best cut out to do is similar to that outlined in the section on German Shorthairs (which they strongly resemble except for a rough coat and whiskered face).

Wirehairs have a clownish streak in them, and are a bit more quick and agile than the Shorthair. Like the Shorthair they make fine dogs for use on commercial shooting establishments, since they'll find and point, and can also be called upon to retrieve, taking to this quite naturally. They also take to water readily, and their coarse coats dry as rapidly as any breed's. Thus they can do some waterfowl work if conditions aren't too severe.

Their range is from close to medium, and most have a more pleasing way of going, and a bit more "hop" (sustained drive off the hindquarters) than that exhibited by many representatives of the other Continental breeds. However, their high-arched foot can get sore if they're hunted extensively in snowy or icy conditions.

They are affectionate and highly intelligent; and while somewhat

"Point" and "Back." This pair of German Wirehaired Pointers shows what finished dogs of the pointing breeds are expected to do. Pointing is *Haar Baron's Mike*, the first GWP to be recognized by the AKC as a Field Champion, and backing is his dam, *Haar Baron's Gremlin*, both a field and bench Champion. They're owned by Cliff Faestel of Brookfield, Wisconsin.

aloof with strangers, they are very demonstrative and affectionate with those they know. Thus they reach fullest development as combination companion and hunting dogs, being happier in the home and around people than in a kennel.

## CHESAPEAKE BAY RETRIEVER

The man looking for a really tough dog, mentally and physically, for work on ducks and geese under the most arduous conditions, will probably settle on a Chesapeake. Possessing a tight, oily coat, backed by a rugged constitution and independent bent of mind, Chesapeakes perform best when the going is roughest.

While primarily a waterfowl dog where the going is wet and cold, the Ches can also be used to retrieve game shot in the uplands, and some can be trained to work out in front and flush upland birds within gun range of the hunter.

Tough as a Marine drill instructor, the Chesapeake is seldom lovable, but he earns respect for his "never-quit" performance of duty under

This Chesapeake will never win any ribbons on the bench, but he's a winner in the big marshes of Manitoba where it takes a lot of dog to retrieve a lot of ducks. He's owned by Bill Hoard of Fort Atkinson, Wisconsin.

conditions that would make other breeds balk. Intelligent but stubborn, he needs a firm hand, and his trainer must be ready to make him back down if he challenges authority. But in matters like marking and retrieving shot birds, his strong natural instincts should be given full rein and he'll produce with a minimum of training. Proper introduction to game will prevent his handling birds too roughly.

The Chesapeake will thus present some training problems, for he is a one-man or one-family dog, and is not particularly sociable with humans or other dogs. However, he is hard to beat for marsh and water work when the chips are down.

## GOLDEN RETRIEVER

It's easy to become enamored of a dog that's both beautiful and capable as a retriever of waterfowl and upland game, and the Golden retriever fits this description. Most will also readily adapt to working within gun range for flushing upland birds, although the striking Golden coat can be a bit of a problem when it loads up with water, mud and sticktights.

The Golden is a "soft" dog, responding best to coaxing and persistent repetition in training. Get too harsh with one, and training will be set back until the dog quits feeling bad or sulking about it. Except for the care the coat requires, the Golden is a wonderful combination of house-dog and hunting companion. With a very affectionate, eager-to-please disposition, he gets along well with other dogs and with all humans.

Seldom is "hard mouth" (too rough handling of birds) any problem with Goldens and they *may* be soft-mouthed to an extreme, requiring some work to get them to take a really firm hold on a bird. Their nose is excellent and they're best as retrievers on upland game or dove shoots.

Though the Golden is capable of doing anything today's waterfowl hunter is going to ask, he has to be rated the least happy and proficient among the retrievers in water work. On the whole, however, he is a joy for man, woman or child to train, being quick to learn and eager to please.

## LABRADOR RETRIEVER

There's good reason why the Labrador is the most popular retriever and a highly favored gun dog. Intelligent, trainable and well-balanced, with a "no-frills" physical appearance, he's a leading candidate for the man seeking a versatile dog.

While rated a waterfowl-fetching specialist, most Labs not only retrieve well on land, but very readily adapt to use as a flushing dog, working within gun range to produce as well as recover upland game.

The alertness and intelligence required by a waterfowl retriever are well displayed by this Labrador Retriever bitch, *Clinker Dhu,* a favorite of the author's.

If a man is toying with the idea of having both a hunting and a field-trial dog, plus a companion around the house, the Lab is a judicious pick. He can be had in any of three colors, black, yellow or chocolate.

The Lab is a good bet for the mixed-bag hunter, who does a lot of waterfowling but also spices things with some pheasant, ruffed grouse and woodcock shooting. Neither as stubborn as the Chesapeake or as eager to please as the Golden, Labs have fire and dash along with intelligent biddability, making for a dog both eager to please, yet independent enough to be interesting and capable.

With a short, clean coat and even disposition, the Lab can be a fine house dog, but he also adjusts well when kenneled, and is sociable with humans and other dogs.

A strong, hardy dog, classy worker and willing learner, Labs can be most easily trained by an amateur, and polished to a high gloss by a professional.

## ENGLISH SETTER

Setter popularity in the field has skidded considerably in the last quarter-century, but they remain beautiful dogs who can produce and point upland game birds "as pretty as a picture."

Specialists, they are second only to the Pointer as the top choice for quail where the country is big, and they rate an edge over the Pointer for the man who likes style and dash but hunts more restrictive coverts for ruffed grouse, woodcock and pheasant.

If the hunter wants his Setter to retrieve, chances are he'll have to force-break him, but there is less tendency toward hard mouth in Setters than in Pointers. Fluid in movement in the field and pretty on point, Setters are also favored fireside companions, being very affectionate and fond of people. They have a softer attitude than most Pointers, and respond to the same type of handling that coaxes the best out of Golden Retrievers.

For all practical purposes there are actually two strains of English Setter. One works in the field; the other poses in a show ring. The big-boned, long-coated statuesque beauty of the shows may have some hunting instinct. But it's a long gamble. For a hunting dog, you'll find yourself better satisfied with the less impressive-appearing, field-type Setter, who can run hard and long and has inherited the nose and instincts of hunting ancestors close up in his pedigree.

## GORDON SETTER

This breed comes close to making the list of unknowns among U. S. hunters. Were it not for the show fancier, it's likely the Gordon would be even rarer.

A bit more independent than the English Setter, Gordon temperament is still "setter-like." They are a bit more ponderous and slower working than the more popular pointing breeds, but they enjoy a very limited vogue as woodcock and ruffed grouse dogs in the East, despite a black-and-tan coat that makes them hard to locate in dense autumn cover.

The Gordon is a beautiful dog, well suited to doubling as a family pet, and he has a small but devoted coterie of followers. However, the breed is in dire need of fanciers who will work toward developing his potential as a hunting dog, and at the present time it is difficult to locate Gordons with good hunting backgrounds.

## IRISH SETTER

The Irish Setter is a beautiful, popular and personable dog. However, finding one that can perform adequately in the field is a problem, and

This is a field-type Irish Setter on point. There's quite a difference between this dog and the type you'll see at bench shows.

chances are that when one is located, his appearance will suffer in comparison with what a good-looking Irishman should look like.

Until about World War II, there were some good Irish gun dogs. They weren't field-trial caliber; but then, few bird hunters, at least in the North, want that type of dog. They were satisfactory shooting dogs and family pets. Their numbers have declined, and the Irish Setter is another breed that remains popular because of appearance in the show ring rather than performance in the game coverts.

Fieldwise, this much can be said for the breed: when a hunter gets a good one, he usually has a gem, a pleasure to shoot over and have around, and an interesting personality. They are long-lived dogs, and a hunter can expect to have an experienced bird dog for a couple years past the time he'd expect to retire another.

When they hunt, their range is comfortable for a foot hunter and they keep track of the handler. Irish Setters may balk at too much pressure and are best led into doing something. Once instilled, things learned are long retained, and the man who can relax and enjoy his dog will get the most out of him.

## AMERICAN WATER SPANIEL

This is one of the most versatile, but generally ignored, breeds of dogs in the nation. This breed and the Chesapeake are the only gun dogs developed exclusively in this country. Relatively small and compact, they are good dogs in a duck skiff where their curly coats protect them from water and cold. The same coats, however, load up with sticktights in the uplands.

A bit sharper in temperament than most spaniels, they still have lovable dispositions and are quick to learn. Because they are not "pretty" dogs, those that exist today are mostly from practical working stock, assuring the purchaser of a pup that his chances are good of getting a trainable one with the right instincts.

They make excellent flush dogs and retrievers of ruffed grouse, woodcock and pheasant, and they're adept in water and marsh, capable of handling virtually any duck hunting chores within the restrictions of present-day season and bag limits. The American Water Spaniel is the answer for a hunter who doesn't specialize in anything in particular, but wants a close-working hunter of feather and fur in the uplands who is also a reliable fetcher of ducks and shorebirds.

American Water Spaniels aren't common dogs in the U.S., but they're proficient hunters and retrievers on land or water. This one holding the mallard is owned by the author's daughter.

## BRITTANY SPANIEL

Tremendous improvement in the hunting qualities of this breed in the past decade has made the Brittany a sensible choice for Eastern and Mid-Western sportsmen who want to use a pointing dog in dense and restricted coverts. The Brittany is the only spaniel that points game.

The Brit is an easy dog to adapt to use in ruffed grouse and woodcock coverts because the breed's natural range is restricted. When similar conditions apply in pheasant hunting they can also rate as topnotch performers on that bird. They are fully capable of handling quail and other game that is found scattered over "big country," but don't possess the range and stamina to qualify as far-reaching covey dogs.

The Brittanys are small, as pointing dogs go, and their temperament is a combination of aloofness and softness which can baffle impatient trainers. This is another breed that responds best to repetitious coaxing rather than harsh discipline.

Brittanys make ideal dogs for the upland hunter who walks and frets if he can't see his dog all the time. Unfortunately some of the breed

Perhaps Brittany Spaniels (like the one above) are small and close-ranging, but they can sure thrill a hunter when they go on point!

are difficult to get out from under foot. On the other hand, field-trial enthusiasts have developed bold, good-ranging Brits that get out to distances that would dismay most practical bird hunters. Fortunately, a happy medium is reached with most of this breed through training, if not by instinct.

## COCKER SPANIEL

This is another popular gun-dog breed which we'd no longer class as a gun dog if our criterion were solely the number used in the hunting field.

Finding a *hunting* Cocker Spaniel, or a pup with a working background, is a tough task. The dogs now produced as a result of show-ring popularity are seldom satisfactory in the field. They are a long way removed from working ancestry, their pop-eyes are vulnerable when working in heavy brush and they're encumbered by uselessly heavy coats and trim.

Nevertheless, a working Cocker shows up once in a while, and their merriness and diligence overcome their size handicap and make them a real joy in the field. They can handle ruffed grouse and woodcock very well and take to retrieving most naturally, both from land and water. However, a mallard or pheasant is a real mouthful for them, and constant use under severe weather and water conditions is expecting too much.

## ENGLISH COCKER SPANIEL

This breed is not common, and probably few casual observers could tell it from a Cocker Spaniel unless they misidentified it as a small English Springer Spaniel. Even so, probably the bulk of the Cockers hunting and competing in field trials today are English Cockers.

Being a bit larger than the Cocker, possessing brows that protect the eyes, and being free from excess feather and coat, English Cockers are more practical field prospects. Merry and animated in the field, they are excellent for flushing and retrieving woodcock and ruffed grouse, and are capable of picking up pheasant and retrieving ducks and shorebirds on occasion. Good natural retrievers for the most part, they need a firm hand in training despite their lovable dispositions, for they will ingratiatingly but stubbornly try to get their own way.

English cocker spaniels aren't seen too often in the field, but good flushers and retrievers like this one can sure afford a lot of pleasure.

Dave Duffey accepts a pheasant from his English Springer Spaniel, *Flirt*.

## ENGLISH SPRINGER SPANIEL

This breed comes as near as any to being capable of performing the general hunting duties that justify a breed's being called an "all-round dog."

The man who hunts a little or a lot of everything, with particular emphasis on pheasant, ruffed grouse and woodcock, plus some work on ducks and shorebirds will find great pleasure in this natural flusher and fetcher of game.

To turn out a really finished dog, as much work must be put in on a Springer as on a pointer or setter. But for the less demanding hunter who just wants to kill some birds, exposure to the game and rudimentary training will usually result in the Springer coming through satisfactorily.

Aggressive on game and merry in action, the Springer is also an affectionate and appreciative family dog which can adapt to virtually any kennel or home situation. Springers want to please, but they also display independence, and have the ability to absorb strict discipline when fairly meted out. Again, this word to the wise: there are show Springers and field Springers. As in the case of the English Setter, these are virtually separate breeds. By all means get your Springer from hunting or field-trial stock. He won't be as big or as pretty, but he will work and be trainable.

The field Springer is large enough to perform virtually any hunting task asked by today's sportsman. He is intelligently trainable, and his happy hustle and desire make him a joy to observe and work with in the field.

## IRISH WATER SPANIEL

Another comparatively rare breed on the U. S. hunting scene, the "rat-tail spaniel" is best appreciated by a certain type of owner, one who possesses a sense of humor and a willingness to concede at times that his dog is smarter than he.

Biggest of the spaniels, the Irish Water is actually a retriever and is entered in retriever trials when he competes (which is seldom). Actually, many members of this breed are just too smart for their own good. Not content to do just what a handler wants them to do, they'll try to find a different way to accomplish it, or throw in some sideline activity for good measure.

Clownish by nature, they are nevertheless very capable water dogs which can be recommended to the waterfowl and shorebird shooter, being large enough and tenacious enough to handle even geese. They can be worked as flush dogs on pheasant, ruffed grouse and woodcock in the uplands, but the very heavy, curly coats attract burrs and sticktights.

Their size and hard-to-manage coats just don't appeal to most home owners, although these dogs are fond of people. But for the man who likes a "different" dog whose appearance will inspire smiles and ques-

This Vizsla is "getting a noseful" during a training session, while an English Setter backs him.

tions, who wants a lot of fun and some capable work on game, regardless of weather or water conditions, the Irisher is a good pick.

## VIZSLA

Another "new" dog on the U. S. hunting scene, the Vizsla (pronounced Veesh-la) was recognized by the AKC in 1960. Of Hungarian origin, the Vizsla's duties are the same as the other Continental pointing breeds: find, point and retrieve game. This is essentially a close-working dog, best adapted to solid rather than scattered cover hunting.

Midwestern hunters, for the most part, are now giving these dogs a try, and an ambitious parent organization stages a national trial for Vizslas once each year. They have little to offer beyond what other breeds in their classification have already established.

However, their yellow color is attractive and they are neat appearing, which can well adapt to home life, and fit in with the hunter who wants a pointing dog he can keep visual and verbal contact with in the field.

A Weimaraner on point.

## WEIMARANER

An unusual breed in more ways than one, the Weimaraner (pronounced Vy-mar-ahner) has a history of over promotion which has
swirled controversy around the breed.

They've been called everything from super-dogs to useless biscuit-
eaters. I'm not listed as an admirer of this breed, but I've seen a few
individuals who were worthwhile field dogs, and satisfactory not only
to their owners but to non-biased hunters. The problem seems to be to
find a capable hunter among numerous dogs represented as such; a
dog about which you can feel quietly and justifiably proud, rather than
one that requires a raft of ingenious excuses in order to explain a lack
of performance. It may be that the problem is owners, outbluffed and
outsmarted by canines, rather than problem dogs.

That the breed is trainable is proven by their work in obedience
trials, and the gun-dog trainer will find them most receptive to militant
and no-nonsense discipline. The Weimaraner can be expected to work
in the same manner as the other Continental breeds, and on the same
game: pheasant, ruffed grouse, woodcock, and to a limited extent,
waterfowl.

# 4

## Matching the Dog
## to the Game

The prime requisite in dog training is to have a dog to train. Which dog you select will be your own choice, dictated by things ranging from the tangible, like size or length of coat, to the intangible, such as the special appeal a specific dog or breed may have.

But we're interested here chiefly in practicality. Which dog is best for the job? This should be the major factor in selecting the dog you're going to spend the next decade or so with, barring unforeseen tragedy.

You may not agree with the advice herein, but it's nonetheless intended to give you an idea of what breed to concentrate on as you seek the dog you are going to train. You may be disconcerted to find that the dog you have selected to do the job you want done just doesn't rate high on my list for that particular job. But this is not intended as a "propaganda piece" to promote a certain breed of dog. It's an honest evaluation of each of the breed's capabilities as to what they do best and what suits them most.

To avoid repeating all the qualifications that necessarily modify any honest evaluation of dogs and of their capabilities and training, let's get one thing out of the way now. In many instances we'll be talking generalities. But sure, there are always exceptions that prove the rule. So don't call me names when I say that an English Pointer is a poor bet as a waterfowl retriever, just because you happen to have one that does a crackerjack job fetching ducks.

Any dog, of any breed, that does well the job he's best suited for is a good dog in my book. The dog that goes beyond these bounds and performs well in a category not expected of him is even more admirable. But you can't count on many members of a given breed doing this, so you play percentages. Only consider those breeds that have already established that most of its members, given proper experience and training, can be expected to do the job you want.

Keep in mind the game you're going to hunt when you try to decide which breeds to concentrate on in making up your mind. In matching the kind of hunting you'll do with the dog you're selecting, remember that there are three different "styles" of hunting in which the breeds specialize: pointing, flushing and retrieving. Because of this, direct comparisons (like saying a Springer Spaniel is a better pheasant dog than an Irish Setter) aren't reasonable. So let's do it by game species, giving every breed a fair shake.

### WATERFOWL

For the man who hunts waterfowl and shorebirds primarily or exclusively, one of the retrievers—Labrador, Golden, Chesapeake, or Irish Water Spaniel—is the only sensible choice. Secondary choices, when working conditions are not too arduous, would be the American Water Spaniel and the English Springer Spaniel. Farther down the line you may even consider the multi-purpose pointing breeds—German Shorthair, German Wirehair, Wirehaired Pointing Griffon, Weimaraner and Vizsla—with the Cocker spaniel rated below the Springer and American Water, chiefly because of lack of size. Very poor bets are the pointers, the three setter varieties, and the Brittany Spaniel.

### PHEASANT

If you want to shoot over a pointing dog, particularly in thick, restricted cover, the Continental (multi-purpose) pointing breeds led by the German Shorthair, the German Wirehair and the Brittany are best bets. In big, relatively open country, the wider-ranging English Setters and Pointers will do a better job. Between these extremes, and trailing as a choice for a pheasant dog, are the Irish and Gordon setters.

A Canada goose is a big burden, even for a large retriever, but this yellow Labrador is determined to drag this big gander in.

Pheasant are also hunted with flush-type dogs, which are more practical as pheasant producers in most instances than the pointing breeds. Here the English Springer rates as tops, and American Waters, Cockers and the four retriever breeds may also perform in exemplary fashion.

Bird shooting in California—an English Springer Spaniel puts up a pheasant from the rice fields.

## RUFFED GROUSE

If you're starting with a raw prospect, and it's a pointing dog you are interested in, the Brittany Spaniel rates as a best bet. Ranking right behind them are English Setters, the German pointers, Pointers and the Irish and Gordon setters, in about that order.

For a majority of ruffed grouse hunters as for pheasant hunters, the flush-type dogs are more practical than pointing dogs, and the choice between spaniels and retrievers is pretty much a tossup with spaniels getting the edge.

The top dog on ruffed grouse is the English Springer Spaniel, and the expression on *Flirt's* face shows how much she likes to retrieve them.

## WOODCOCK

The statements applied to dogs used on ruffed grouse also apply here, even though woodcock react to dogs differently, and hold very well for the pointing breeds. Both game birds are frequently found in the same cover and under the same conditions, usually necessitating a dog working both species. Wide-ranging pointing dogs are worse than worthless in grouse and woodcock cover.

## BOBWHITE QUAIL

For getting the most out of quail hunting, pointing dogs should receive virtually the only consideration. Top choice is the Pointer, particularly in big plantation-type country, closely followed by the English Setter. In more restricted coverts, the German breeds, the Brittany and the Irish and Gordon setters can be the ticket.

Big-going Pointers are unsurpassed for quail hunting, and they're *the* bird dogs in the South. This is 1964 National Champion *War Storm,* owned by B. McCall of Birmingham, Alabama.

Flushing dogs are a poor choice for quail hunting. However, in the North in bitter cold weather, when birds must be rooted out of dense cover, a spaniel or retriever can do a fine job within its own limitations.

## SHARPTAIL GROUSE, PRAIRIE CHICKEN, HUNGARIAN PARTRIDGE

It would be cutting it pretty fine to differentiate between the dog work desired on these game species and quail. So the statements about bobwhites also generally apply here. The choice is one of the pointing breeds.

## CHUKAR PARTRIDGE, DESERT QUAIL

Few are the dogs of any breed that work these birds well, so no firm recommendation can be made; but a good retriever seems as practical as any, and can insure recovery of long and difficult falls.

## DOVE

This is all retrieving work, so the Lab, Golden, Chesapeake and Irish Water rate the edge, although they may be pushed by Springer, Cocker and American Water spaniels, and a good retriever among the Shorthairs, Weimaraners, Wirehairs, and Vizslas can't be ruled out.

Summed up, it's best to go with the retrievers for waterfowl; spaniels for ruffed grouse, woodcock and pheasant; and one of the pointing breeds for quail, sharptail, chicken and Hun.

But what about the dog for the man who does a bit of everything—the man looking for a combination dog, or one of those non-existent "all-rounders?"

A dual job commonly asked of a dog is hunting both waterfowl and pheasant. You'll have to make your own choice among Chesapeakes, Labradors, Goldens and Irish Waters, which you'll find best in the water and under the toughest elemental conditions. Among these retrievers, Labradors and Goldens best adjust to the upland end of the work. But if the emphasis is strong on pheasant with quite a bit of duck hunting thrown in, the Springer or the American can do the job.

In any upland gunning which features birds in "big country," with scattered patches of cover where you can follow a wide-ranging dog and keep visual track of him, the Pointer and English Setter are un-excelled. If the country is restricted and the cover dense, and it's work to keep track of a "big-going" dog, then the Brittany, German Short hair and German Wirehair are the answer.

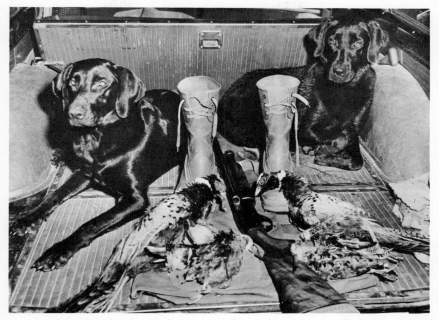

A pair of tired Labradors belonging to the author take a well-deserved break after producing a mixed bag of pheasant and woodcock.

Should hunting consist of lots of pheasant shooting, with some good grouse and woodcock hunting tossed in, along with a bit of duck hunting, Springer and American Water spaniels top the list. Labrador Retrievers can also do this job, and if most of the emphasis is on the uplands with waterfowl retrieving only on rare occasions, German Shorthairs and Wirehairs are also fine, particularly if the hunter takes occasional jaunts for quail, prairie grouse or Hun.

If consistent performance is of more interest to you than the thrill a pointing dog provides when he locks up on birds or the relatively easier shooting it affords, the closest thing to an all-around dog, that will find and flush game within range and also fetch it back to you after you've shot it, is the English Springer Spaniel, followed by the other spaniel and retriever breeds.

Since there have been some pretty dogmatic (no pun intended) statements made here, it's only fair that an explanation be given for the recommendations, to indicate why some breeds have been mentioned more prominently than others.

This will probably cause some readers to throw this book across the room, simply because they couldn't disagree with me more. But I warned you I'd be controversial. My purpose is to help the would-be dog trainer, not to sell or promote any specific breed. At the time of writing I have nine different breeds in my kennel and home, and I've had many others and will have still more. I'm interested only in how the dog does his job, not what color or breed he is.

Of the retriever breeds, the Labrador is the most adaptable to a variety of jobs and conditions; the Chesapeake is a wonder when conditions are arduous, and is unsurpassed for water work; the Golden is wonderfully lovable in temperament, learns quickly and is better on land than in water; the Irish Water Spaniel takes a back seat to no dog in the marsh, but there are too few working today to make complete evaluation possible.

The best of the pointers are often just too much dog for the cover they are asked to work, and to a lesser extent this is also true of English Setters. Conversely, in many instances the Continental pointing breeds are just not enough dog for the big country they may be put down in. I've tried to consider the game and conditions as they generally exist, and the dogs that normally do the best under these average conditions.

The German Shorthair and the Brittany have both proven themselves, with the Shorthair virtually setting the standard for performance among the Continental breeds, and the Brittany having made great strides

Among the pointing breeds, German Shorthaired Pointers are a good bet for working ruffed grouse, and this pair puts on a fine demonstration of how grouse can be handled, on occasion, by a pointing dog.

Pointing dogs that handle ruffed grouse well are always hard to come by, but Brittany Spaniels like the one shown above often handle this game very well.

in the past two decades. The German Wirehair is now proving out very well; the Wirehaired Pointing Griffon (sometimes confused with the German Wirehair) is rare but may be catching on. The Vizsla is no longer rare, but the jury is still out on the breed's ability in general. The Weimaraner hasn't yet measured up to exaggerated claims made for it. Good-hunting Irish Setters are rare, although a field type is being developed. The Gordon Setter is even less common afield.

Among the spaniels, the English Springer has far and away proven its worth; the American Water is capable, and while lacking the fire and dash of a good Springer he may be just what a more leisurely hunter wants. Not many hunting strains of American Cocker are available and its small size is a hindrance; and while the English Cocker has possibilities, with most cockers in the field being of this breed, it is still a rare hunting dog.

Pointers and setters may be difficult to train when it comes to soft-mouthed retrieving, and seldom are they the accurate markers that spaniels and retrievers are. The Continental breeds take to retrieving more readily than the other pointing dogs, and are required to "fetch" as part of their field trial work.

Many retrievers, with their long heritage of complete subservience to the handler, will lack the initiative to get out and work in front of the gun. Spaniels just won't thrill the man who likes to have his game pointed and many may be too eager in their application, running birds up out of range if not controlled.

This is a brief and as plain as I can say it, bearing in mind that most of these weaknesses can be overcome to a large extent with proper training. But picking the right dog with the right instincts makes the training so much easier and quicker that a prospective dog owner should appreciate a little "Dutch-uncle" talk.

One more point. Maybe you have it in the back of your mind that the dog you pick will be not only your personal gun dog, but may turn into a field-trial performer as well. While this is unlikely, it's certainly not impossible. So if the field-trial bug bites you or has already nipped you, again play the percentages. The percentages say it's the Pointer in the major bird-dog circuit, the German Shorthair in the "shoot-to-kill" trials for the Continental pointing breeds, and the Labrador in the retriever trials. Springers are the only spaniels for which significant numbers of trials are held.

I've tried to help you select the breed best suited to you and to the job you've laid out for your dog, via the above comments on the temperaments, abilities, and physical characteristics of the various breeds.

So now you've made up your mind. You have the right dog—you think. Or maybe my opinion about a dog you already have has disappointed or angered you. In any case, it's now time to get into the matter of "How can I train this paragon (or lunkhead), to get the best out of his natural instincts, and make the most of what I've got?"

That's where we're going now, friend, following a short explanatory chapter which may salve your ego. For you ought to know one thing before embarking on this venture: WHEN A DOG DOESN'T TURN OUT WELL, IT'S NOT ALWAYS THE TRAINER'S FAULT.

# 5

## The Four Classes
## of Dogs

Not all dogs are good dogs.

I don't mean to belabor the obvious. For you've certainly run across enough damn-fool, scatter-brained, incapable and worthless mutts, both in the field and in the home, to far outnumber those wonderfully "savvy" dogs that know their way around, and that you'd hand over a fair share of your income to buy.

But if you listen to a lot of people talk, or read books about dogs written by some rara avis who purports to know more about dogs and love them more than people, you'll reach the conclusion that there are no bad dogs, just bad trainers. "Don't blame poor little Fido. Blame his owner for his faults."

This is hogwash! Without discounting the effect of environment one bit, it's fair to say that some good hunting dogs are born, not made. In human terms it takes more than environment to turn out either an upstanding citizen or a juvenile delinquent, and so it is with dogs. Sometimes it's just a matter of finding the proper niche or the right approach: if a dog has the proper instincts when it's whelped, it's the responsibility of the trainer to channel these properly. But some dogs are impossible. An experienced trainer will recognize this and get rid of the dog. An *in*experienced one will blame himself, downrate his own ability and maintain the worthless canine in high style, because he feels guilty about not doing right by the dog.

Over the years, I've come up with four classifications for dogs, regardless of breed. There are: 1. Great dogs, 2. Naturally good dogs, 3. Made dogs, and 4. Palookas. The latter simply are not worth messing with. They seem to have a fabulous collection of mismated nuts and bolts rattling around between their ears, and they're worthless as hunters, pets, or in most cases, even as show dogs.

The truly great dogs are the result of fortunate inheritance and superior training and handling, plus plenty of experience. As a rule

When ducks are down in rough, mucky going, a good retriever like this Golden will pay you back with interest for the time you spent in training him.

the great dogs are just too much dog for most people and can be utilized to the fullest by only a few, while the palookas are a waste of time, money and patience for everyone.

That leaves us with the pair of classifications inbetween, the "naturally good dogs" and the "made dogs," which come in various overlapping shades.

"Naturally good dogs" are the ones who become satisfactory hunters with a modicum of training and experience, or can be real "brag" dogs if they get into the hands of someone who knows a bit about bringing out the best in a dog, and gives it opportunities to work.

"Made dogs," as the term implies, are virtually fashioned by a man or men. They may lack many of the extra "somethings" that make a dog click right, but possess *some* good qualities and ability, and willingness to learn. In a competent trainer's hands he becomes an acceptable dog, perhaps one that's hard to tell from a naturally good dog. In the hands of a man with a shortage of time and know-how, the potential "made dog" drops down into the "palooka" class.

There has been a spate of dog writing based on a new theory that all you have to do is get a dog of good breeding at an early age, follow a certain procedure and you'll have yourself a trained dog. This theory has merit. And it works with the right dog. But only a minority of

The intensity of this German Shorthaired Pointer tells his master he's got birds, right now and right *there!*

first-time dog owners will be lucky enough to hit this easily-trained dog. The majority are going to have to know what to do when they hit a snag, or encounter a dog that is a bit slow in coming around.

This book is not going to deal with problem dogs. They are best gotten rid of, or turned over to a good professional. But we will deal with the more common bugs in a dog's mental make-up, that occur among dogs with the potential to be "made" into hunting companions you won't have to apologize for.

At one time or another many dog owners have to face up to the question of whether a dog is worth spending more time and money to develop. This book should help you decide. The response of all dogs will vary somewhat, the naturally good ones catching on quickly, and others—the made ones—coming a bit more slowly. But if the methods outlined here as standard procedure plus the suggestions for dealing with specific problems don't work after you've given them an honest try, start over with a more promising prospect.

There's no point in kidding ourselves about another thing. Just as not every dog is a good dog, neither is every man a good trainer. So soaking up what this book offers doesn't guarantee you'll turn out the dog of your dreams. Just as there are puppies who seem to be "born knowing," there are humans who have a "sixth sense" when it comes

The Brittany Spaniel is a good gun dog for the hunter who goes afoot, and it can readily be taught to retrieve shot game as well as to point it.

to handling animals. They seldom have problem dogs, while another man never has a good one.

You're also going to hear a lot of references to "giving the dog a chance" or giving him experience. The fact is that you can yard-train and obedience-train to perfection, but only experience on actual game will make a truly fine hunting dog. In many instances, if the pup has the right instincts, and is given a chance to find out what the game is all about, he'll produce birds for you even though his training has been slipshod and his manners leave something to be desired. And that, after all is the essence of the game. All else is refinement.

This book should help you understand not only *what to do* in training a dog, but *why* you do it. Everyone does a better job if he knows the reason a certain procedure is utilized. But neither this book, nor any other one can do it all for you. You have to help.

"Helping" means spending time with your dog, and often using your ingenuity to deal with something not specifically covered in the book. Nor can I emphasize too much the actual field work, where a dog gets the scent, sight and sound of game. And finally, hunt him, every chance you get, even though he may not be completely trained. For nothing beats bird-shooting over a dog for making him a keen, never-quit, knowledgeable hunting companion.

With this cooperation on your part, the following chapters will help give you the kind of dog that will prompt strangers to ask, "Did you really train that dog yourself?"

It's that kind of question that makes a man's shirt buttons pop and his hat-band tighten, when he can answer in the affirmative. So get on with it.

# 6

## *Seven Positive Training Rules*

A covey of bird-dog trainers, just down from the Canadian prairies, were munching sandwiches when I hunkered down against the side of the car. The U. S. Chicken Championship, a major field trial run on sharptailed grouse and prairie chicken near Solon Springs, Wisconsin, had been interrupted for the midday lunch break.

"Gonna be here for the whole trial, Duff?" one asked.

I shook my head. "Nope, just for the day. Partridge and woodcock season opened up over the weekend, and I'm up for the hunting."

"What you got for dogs?" the trainer asked.

"Four different ones," I answered. "A Pointer, a German Wirehair, a Labrador and a Springer Spaniel."

A veteran of the bird-dog wars looked up and in slow Louisiana-accented measure began a tale. "Ah trained me one of those Springuhs once," he said. "Most damned embarrassin' thing ever happened at me."

"This was away back in the thuhties," he continued. "Fellah come in with this dawg—kinda a showt-tailed settuh, lahk. He says, 'Thisye is a Springuh Span'l. Train him foh me.' Damndest job Ah evuh unduh-took. But Ah fahnally got the son of a gun to pointin'. Called the man,

46

tol' him to come get his dawg. Ah took the dawg out on buhds to show him—pretty proud o' mahse'f—and that little ol' dawg come on point jus' as nahce as yuh please. But his ownuh wa'n't pleased. No suh! He lahked to blowed his stack. 'Yew done ruin't mah dawg!' he holluhed. Don't have to tell yew that's the fu'st and last Springuh Ah evah trained."

I recite this anecdote to illustrate a couple of things. First, all dogs are not designed or intended for the same thing, and secondly, even professionals can make an error, particularly when they are specializing, as many are, in handling a certain type of dog. So you don't have to be ashamed of your mistakes. Everybody makes 'em. Find out what's right and you can correct them.

Having read this far, you already know more than that particular dog man knew at that stage of his experience, namely that Springer Spaniels are not pointing dogs. But before snickering too loud at the professional's dilemma, don't forget that it illustrates another point. Regardless of the dog's natural bent, he can be handmade into doing a lot of things if the trainer knows what he is doing and works at it.

Some generalities must be grasped by the would-be trainer before he can become specific. You've read a general outline of how a retriever, a spaniel and a pointing dog are expected to work. A bit further on you'll get into the methods used in training dogs in each of these classifications, with sidelights on what to expect and how to treat various breeds included in each group.

Meanwhile, there are seven positive rules that apply to all dogs, whether they're intended for hunting, working or just companionship. Keep these in mind and you can make all kinds of trivial errors and still come up with a well-trained dog.

1. Tell a dog. Don't ask him.
2. Be consistent.
3. Give a command only when you are prepared to enforce it.
4. Punish only when the dog understands what the punishment is for.
5. But *do* punish when a dog has learned a command but defies you.
6. Praise lavishly when a dog does right.
7. Never fool your dog.

There are those who would address a dog in dulcet tones even when old Spot has committed some unpardonable sin. Some people can actually train a dog that way, never losing their temper, never raising their voice—so they tell me.

I can't. I holler, and what I holler isn't always acceptable in polite society. But how else are you going to get the attention of a hard-headed little bitch who decides she's going to go with her birds when she's

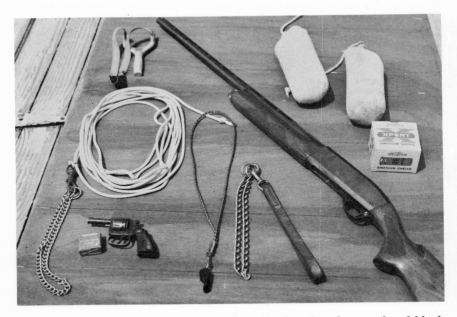

Here's the equipment a dog trainer needs to do the job right: pistol and blank
cartridges, slip-chain collar with check rope, slingshot, whistle, slip-chain
collar with short leash, shotgun with shells and retrieving dummies.

half-a-quarter away from you? Or a lackadaisical Labrador pup that
decides he'll investigate every damn decoy in the stool before heading
out for the crippled canvasback that's trying to make open water?

Believe me, brother, few are the dogs you and I will encounter
that won't at one time or another be begging to be bellered at. You
have my permission to do it. It'll do both you and the dog some good.
Even in less trying straits, when volume isn't a requirement, snap
out the commands incisively, so the dog knows you aren't just conversing
with him. Tell him. Don't ask him.

Consistency means just that. Don't punish a dog for something one
day, and let him get away with it the next. You can't deviate. It's
either right or wrong.

When you give a command, see that it's obeyed. A dog in training
is like a child. He'll push your patience as far as he can for as long
as he can get away with it. That's why patience is not on my list of
requirements for a successful dog trainer. Persistency, yes. But patience,
no. Sometimes anger and impatience, properly directed, pay off.

Depending on the dog's response to commands, praise or punishment
can work wonders in impressing him with what you want him to do.

This includes encouragement when he does something good on his own hook, without any command from you. When he's busily snuffling bird scent, tell him what a good boy he is, and egg him on. Always encourage him if his reaction to something new and strange is good; ignore if it's bad. Punishing him because his reaction is wrong to something new is worse than senseless. He may connect this new experience with the punishment.

Always go to your dog—no matter where he may be—to honor the find he makes on birds.

So if your young dog has never had any basic training in fetching dummies and birds, for example, and you whale him because he doesn't jump right in and fetch the first duck you knock down opening day, you're not only going to complicate your training job, but you may wind up with a dog who wants nothing to do with the game or the goal.

But DO punish when a dog has demonstrated he knows what is expected of him but refuses to do it. Not only must the punishment match the offense (a sharp swat if he doesn't sit with alacrity vs. a sound thrashing for chewing up a bird, for example) but it must match the dog's temperament. Just a harsh word or two may be all a "soft" dog requires. A tough one may respond to little less than a heavy belt, laid on heavily. In this matter you must use judgment, as you best understand your own dog.

When licking a recalcitrant canine, however, keep one thing in mind. The first three or four swats are for the dog's good. Anything beyond that you're doing for your own satisfaction.

By lavish praise, I mean making a fuss over him. By all means talk to him. Just as you give him commands in a sharp, firm voice, when he does the job right you should sweet-talk him. You'll be surprised how well a dog responds to sweet talk. After a dog is fully trained, a quiet word or two and a warm pat will suffice as a reward. But while he's being trained, lay it on.

A dog must trust you. So don't fool him. Don't ever send him out with a command to retrieve if there's nothing there for him to fetch. Don't tell him "birds, birds, hunt 'em out" in a place devoid of game. Do these things only when there is an object to retrieve (and make sure he gets it even if it means guiding him out to it), or when you know there is a bird or scent in the cover.

If he's never been fooled, it's remarkable how quickly a dog will associate the excited urgency of the command with the thing or things he gets praised for and will redouble his efforts to seek and produce.

So on to the specifics of training the retriever, the spaniel and the pointing dog.

# 7

# *Retriever Training*

Because retrieving is both their business and their instinctive inheritance, the Labrador, Golden, Chesapeake and Irish Water puppy need learn only three other things before they start training for what will be their life's work and pleasure.

The pup must know his name. This will alert him to the fact that you want his attention, and obedience to a subsequent command. It will also be used later in the training to send the dog to retrieve.

He should also be taught the command "No!"—meaning to cease and desist doing whatever he happens to be doing that you don't want him to.

Finally, he should come when called. I use the command "Here!" You may prefer to say "Come!" or use any other word you desire to get the idea across, as long as it's short, and the only one used to demand that he do this.

Your pup need not be particularly well-versed in even these three commands before you start the retrieving end of his training. You start play-training your puppy from the time you get him, at the age of seven to twelve weeks. This is the best time to acquire a pup, for

51

This pair of Labrador puppies finds it a bit easier to share the dummy, in a play-training session in the water.

a puppy will start learning from about seven weeks on, whether he's taught by a human or learns from good and bad experiences, from his dam or his littermates.

It's best that your retriever learn from you the things you want of him. So get him when he's about two to three months old, and start training immediately.

"Whoa, now!" someone is sure to say. "Such and such a trainer and such and such a book said the time to start training is about seven months (or ten months, or a year, or a year and a half). You calling people liars?"

Nope.

There's really no conflict between this early-training advice and that handed out for years by competent trainers, although many writers have failed to explain it.

What the man means when he says "wait until the dog is more mature" is that the dog is then ready for SERIOUS training, when pressure will be applied.

With these very young pups, I'm talking about PLAY training— the soft sell, if you will, vs. the hard sell. The puppy *thinks* it's play and may even conclude that this is all his own idea. In the course of this "playing" the pup is going to form good habits. What's more, you'll have fun teaching him.

Most important, you'll have your pup ready for some actual hunting by the time he's seven or eight months old, rather than just starting his training then, and you'll have a better dog. It may come even earlier with the precocious ones, somewhat later with the slower ones.

What you are doing is channeling the pup's instincts. This will become habit as quickly as the individual pup is capable of assimilating this guidance. Then by the time you start *demanding* obedience and manners, rather than requesting them, you'll be way ahead of the game, for the pup's responses will already have been established.

Everything you do with a puppy from the age of two months on, and every experience he has, is actually training. This applies to early introduction to water, gunfire, automobiles, people, birds—the works. Remember only that up to the age of about five or six months, you'll have to be happy with what he's coaxed to do right and persistent enough to overcome the things he does wrong.

## NAME

Teaching a dog his name comes almost naturally. Every time you talk to the pup, use his name—whether you're praising, scolding or just greeting him. Repetition is one "secret" of dog training, and a pup hearing his name over and over again will come to recognize it.

## NO

The pup begins to learn the meaning of "No!" from the first time he gets into something you want him out of. The command should be sharp and emphatic in tone. A light swat on the flank or a finger tap on the muzzle won't harm him, and will show him that you mean business. Since most puppies will chew on anything available (including your hand or pants leg) from the time you get him, you can utilize these transgressions to teach him "No!" Every time he starts gnawing, tap or slap him lightly with your hand or a rolled newspaper, and say, "No!" You'll be surprised how quickly he'll halt this activity upon command alone.

In dog training, always try to kill as many birds as possible with one stone. The above is one example of "doubling up." At the same time he is learning a command, the pup is also being taught that biting and chewing are not acceptable activities.

## COMING WHEN CALLED

Again, this is a big game—at first. Puppies are usually looking for something to do. They also possess an instinct to chase anything that moves away from them. Get the pup's attention by calling his name. Then keep calling it and run away from him, clapping your hands and repeating, "Here, Rip! Here, Rip! Here, Rip!" He'll chase you and you let him "catch you." Then praise and sweet-talk him.

You may even be able to get away with remaining stationary, squatting down and calling the pup to you in the same coaxing manner. Give him a tidbit if you wish when he comes, but verbal and manual praise are usually sufficient. The use of the hands is important in training a dog. At this stage he'll learn that they can praise and caress as well as punish and restrain.

Every time you bring his food—and pups up to four months of age should be fed three to four times daily—call him to you *and* the food. He'll associate only pleasantness with this command. When he's older and defies or ignores you during a serious training session, and it's necessary to plink him with a marble from a slingshot or splatter him with a handful of gravel or a snowball, he'll come running *to* you for solace, rather than away from you in fright.

The handclapping does more than just keep his attention riveted on you. It accustoms him to sharp noises. So does banging and dropping his feed pan. He'll learn that noises won't hurt and may even mean fun and praise. This goes a long way in helping to introduce him to strange situations, including gunfire.

Time is an important element. Three ten-minute sessions with your pup or even less will bring better results than one thirty-minute period. A pup's span of interest is short, so don't overdo one exercise; work on several at the same time. Here's where you start training to retrieve, during play-training. Mix it in with the other stuff you're doing now as well as the more advanced things we'll be getting to shortly.

## BEGINNING RETRIEVING

With a small pup, a soft object he can easily carry is the first thing he should be "worked on." An old glove or sock serves very well; knotting the sock works best. Tease the pup with it by sliding it around on the floor in front of him, and get him to try to grab it. Then skid it across the floor, so that he can see it go and follow it. Short tosses will come later; skid it just a couple of feet at first. He'll go after it and grab it. The distance can be increased a bit each session.

Then call his name and coax him to you as you squat down, introducing a new command: "Here, Rip. Fetch!" "Here, Rip. Fetch!" In time you'll be able to dispense with the "Here!"

When he brings the object to you or near you, take it from him firmly but gently and tell him to "Drop!" Don't tug or wrestle with him for it. If he refuses to let go, hold the object in one hand and slide the thumb of your other hand into his mouth, pressing his lower lip against his teeth and squeezing just enough to make him release the object, repeating "Drop!" or "Drop it!" all the while. Then praise him. Don't pull or pry. Simply pinch his lip against his teeth.

Keep repeating this performance, sliding and later tossing the object, saying "Rip! Fetch!" in encouraging tones, and fussing over him when he does it. Five or six "retrieves" a session are plenty. Do it once or several times a day, whenever and wherever you have time. You'll be surprised how quickly this little pup will be scampering after every object you sling along the floor, and proudly returning it to you.

Always squat or kneel when working with a very young pup. It seems to instill confidence, and the pup is more willing to approach you when you're down nearer his level. Start this training inside a building, whether kitchen, garage, basement or some other confined area where distractions are at a minimum and the surroundings familiar. Once he gets it down pat in these surroundings you can move outside to do your work.

When a retriever pup is big enough—three to four months—you can substitute a retrieving dummy (a small, kapok boat fender is excellent) for the glove or sock. It's also smart to save some game-bird wings from your hunting trips. Alternate these with the glove and sock. This way the pup gets accustomed to picking up feathers at an early age. It saves time later on, and makes introduction to birds a simple matter. When you switch to dummies, wings can be taped onto the dummies, increasing the experience the pup has in handling feathers, and familiarizing him with the scent of some of the game he'll be asked to work.

If you have a pup that's too small to take out when the hunting season is on, bring home intact smaller game birds like quail, woodcock or ruffed grouse, and toss them for the pup to retrieve once he's learned to pick up what you toss out.

It may take a little encouragement on your part to get him to pick up this new thing, but if he's done well on gloves, socks, dummies and wings, he'll do it. Don't use a large bird like a pheasant or duck. You can use their wings, however.

Now you can start giving him a "toughie" (as it will be for one of

Retrievers have to learn to sit and hold dummies (which may be plain, or wrapped with bird wings) as this young Chesapeake and Labrador are doing in an off-season training session.

his tender weeks). Put an object out a little distance from him (*not* throwing it so that he sees it) and tell him "Rip, Fetch!" If you make a tossing motion with your arm, he'll probably turn and go a little way looking for something to fetch. It should be in plain sight, and not more than five of six feet from his starting point. If he doesn't find it, but spins around and is confused, walk towards the object to be retrieved, gesticulating with your hand and repeating encouragingly, "Rip, Fetch! Rip, Fetch!" and so on.

But don't ever let him fail to bring in something, once you've told him to fetch. Nothing succeeds like success! If a pup is allowed to fail and go about his play while you pick up, it will set his training back, and lead to his doing a half-hearted job and quitting on rough retrieves when he gets older.

Also, don't ever forget that you are instilling patterns of behavior in this pup which he'll follow when he's older. If the patterns are bad, they'll be hard to eradicate or correct. If they're good, you'll find yourself saying, "that son of a gun seems to train himself."

So even if you have to walk right up to the dummy (wing, bird or whatever you use) and point it out to the pup, guide him up there and have *him* pick it up. Then trot away from him and call him to you as you would when he makes a normal retrieve. Praise him when he picks it up, and when he brings it.

The remaining six of the "Ten Commandments" for puppies can be worked into the training sessions as soon as the pup has the general idea and responds fairly well to "Name," "No," "Here" and "Fetch." These can be safely added provided that you continue to work on the first four, not letting up until you're surprised and disappointed when he *doesn't* obey, rather than just pleased when he *does,* as you must be when you start.

Once he masters the remaining six "Commandments," your dog is likely to be the best-trained canine in the neighborhood—and this at an age when some will claim a dog is only ready to *start* his training. The final six are "Drop," "Sit," "Wait," "Kennel," "Heel" and "Hunt 'em out."

Once he's got these you'll be able to take him almost anywhere you want to go; he'll be ready for the rigors of serious retriever training; and, following proper introduction to gunfire, he'll even be ready to be taken afield on a real hunt. Depending upon your diligence and your pup's precocity, this will happen somewhere between five months and one year of age, with seven to eight months a good general average.

## DROP

This command has probably already been three-quarters or fully learned if your pup is retrieving according to the schedule outlined previously. But I'll repeat. All you do is command "Drop!" several times, as you take the retrieved object from the pup's mouth. If he wants to hang on and won't let go, grasp the object with the left hand and the pup's lower jaw with the right, and slide your right thumb into his mouth, pressing that lower lip against his teeth. He won't bite. But he will open his mouth to relieve the pressure you've applied, and you can take the dummy. Chances are that by the time he's made a couple dozen retrieves he'll be releasing on command.

## SIT

Like humans, retrievers do a lot of their work from a sitting position, so this is vital. To teach a dog to sit on command, simply put your left hand flush against the juncture of the pup's neck and chest (to keep him from moving ahead), straddle his hips with your right thumb and forefinger, and squeeze a bit and push down, saying "Sit!" This forces him into a sitting position. Then praise him.

It will speed things up if you start this after he's done some fetching or playing, and some of the steam that prompts him to wiggle and cavort is expended. If he's a little tired, so much the better. But if he's *too* tired, he may try to sprawl rather than assume a sitting position, and it can be a tougher proposition to jack him up than to plunk him down. After several sessions, when he's dropping well without much resistance to your hand pressure, try saying "Sit!" without using your hands.

Surprise, surprise! He did it! You can't help fussing over him, can you?

What if he didn't do it? Relax, that's normal. But bring those hands into play again. Say "Sit!" and firmly sit him down. Then praise him. Pretty quickly he'll be doing this without manual aid. But sometimes he'll ignore the command and don't let him get away with it! Always force him down if he doesn't sit voluntarily. It won't be long before he'll plunk his fanny down when you say "Sit!" with no assistance from you.

This is the point at which you order "Sit!" and in conjunction with the verbal command, thrust your arm upright, index finger pointed heavenward. This is not a baffled dog trainer's request for some divine assistance; it's the first *hand signal* a dog learns. As soon as he connects the gesture with the verbal command to sit, he'll start sitting on gesture alone. If he doesn't, tell him to "Sit!" and make him sit. Once he's got this, he's taken the first step toward being a dog you can direct by hand signals.

He can learn his first response to a whistle signal in much the same way. Start trilling or "beep, beep, beep," beeping on your whistle in conjunction with your verbal "Here!" command. Pretty soon he's coming to the whistle alone. Why bother with a whistle? It's sharper, more precise, saves your voice and is not as disturbing to game in the field as is a human voice.

The whistle signal to sit is one sharp blast. The training procedure is to say "Sit!" while simultaneously raising your arm and hitting the whistle once. In a short while your dog will plunk his tail down at the proper verbal, whistle or hand signal. After he's mastered this at your side or in a confined area, let him get away from you a little and work on him so he'll sit on command even when he's some distance away. If he refuses when he's a little away from you, DON'T CALL HIM IN and then make him sit. GO TO HIM and plunk him down in the spot he was in when you signalled.

To make maximum use of training time, and to instill good habits once a pup sits on verbal command, put him in a sitting position at your side each time before you throw his fetching dummy. He'll come to associate starting his retrieves from a sitting position, and the fact that sitting eventually leads to fun (retrieving should be the thing a retriever likes to do most) will add spice to the training routine. This way you'll have a dog plunking down with that "what's the next goodie, boss?" expression, rather than one that sulkily performs a chore he's required to. Not that you aren't requiring all these things. But everyone likes a happy worker, including the guy doing the job.

## WAIT

The purpose of this command is to keep a dog "steady" or glued to one spot, and with retrievers this is usually done with the dog in a sitting position.

Eventually this can keep your dog from jumping out of a boat every time you shoot, halt his chase of a missed bird in the uplands, allow you to set him out on a muskrat house where he can see while you take cover to ambush some ducks, or hold him in one spot when you leave him, among many other things. If you want to use the word "Whoa" or "Stay Put" or even "By Golly" it's okay. Just so that what you say means "stay put" to the dog.

He can learn this in either of two ways, or by both. During fetching practice, have him sit. Hold him with your right hand by his collar or the scruff of his neck. Toss the dummy with your left hand (reverse procedure if the dog is on your left side). Quickly grab him with both hands and restrain firmly, saying "Wait!" At first you needn't push him back into sitting position; let him stand, which he'll do as he starts toward the dummy. Align him in the right direction and don't restrain for more than a couple of seconds at first, and then say "Rip, Fetch!" and let him go.

DO NOT DO THIS UNTIL YOUR PUP IS CRAZY ABOUT FETCH-ING. You don't want him to get the idea that you are *against* fetching. You're teaching him a new command. So when you first start this, the restraint time should be minimal. Then gradually hold him a bit longer, until you can take your hands off him and he'll hesitate, waiting for the "Rip, Fetch!" command. Eventually, you'll be able to say "Sit! Wait!" and he'll stay in sitting position until sent.

The more formal introduction to "waiting" is probably better and safer, from the standpoint of not interfering with his desire to retrieve. For the one thing you want, above all else, is a "retrieving maniac."

Sit your dog. Get as far away from him as you can, still keeping one restraining hand on him, repeating "Wait! Wait! Wait!" all the while. This is not a sharp, but a soothing, steadying command at this stage, and it should come out, "Wayyt! "Wayyt! Wayyt!" If he tries to follow or move away, plunk him back in position and sharply command, "Sit! Wait!" Keep this up until you can take your hand off of him, or even straighten up before he moves. When he does, put him back in position and command, "Sit! Wait!"

When he'll stay put until you've straightened up, keep your arm upright with the cautioning finger pointing skyward, still cautioning "Wait!" if he indicates he's going to move, and then quickly release him from control with a command like "All right!" or "Okay!" and call him to you for praising and petting. Don't make him hold too long at first. But keep prolonging the time, backing away a step or two at a time, hand in the air indicating "Sit!" and gradually he'll be staying put even without verbal cautioning.

Once he's pretty solid, tempt him by turning your back, walking around him, etc., always ordering "Wait!" if he acts as if he's going to move out. If he does move out before you've said "All Right!", firmly take him back to his position and start over. When he waits until released, let him know how pleased you are. In a short time you'll be able to walk around him and his head will swivel watching you, or he may shift his butt a bit for a better look, but he won't leave the designated spot, even when you duck out of sight for a moment or two.

Not only has he learned the most important step in being "steady," but he's picked up an extra word in his vocabulary: "All Right!" which means "school's out."

## HEEL

This means "walk attentively by my side until I give you a command to do something else." A dog at heel should always be under control, and the proper execution of this command is useful, in too many ways to enumerate, when it's impractical for the dog to be running about on his own volition and his master wants him with him.

Before this is started, the pup should be introduced to collar and leash. Get a small puppy collar and put it on the pup, letting him wear it until he accepts it—a few minutes a day at first, for hours later on. Attach a long leash or a length of rope to it, and walk with him on it. He'll tug and tangle and fight, but give him plenty of leeway and he'll soon learn that it's futile to fight this gentle restraint. Guide him generally in the direction you want to go. Don't let him get frantic, but do show him that if he's reasonable, things aren't so bad.

Once he's accustomed to the mild restraint of the "long lead" and accepts the fact that his freedom extends only to where the collar tightens, you'll be able to tie him up, when necessary, without a great deal of anxiety. At this point you can get rid of the leather puppy collar, and get a slip-chain collar and a short leash.

I would not attempt to teach heeling before the age of four months, and five to six months is better. This will be the pup's first taste of comparatively harsh restraint, for there is no really efficient way of play-training a dog into heeling. So he should be physically and mentally big enough to take it, and have developed a confidence in and affection for his handler.

Which side he heels on isn't important, but since the right seems most practical to me for a hunting dog, that's what we'll assume. Sit your dog at your right side as in a retrieving position and attach the leash to the slip-chain collar. Then say, "All right, Heel!" and step off. If the pup dashes ahead, jerk him back, saying "Heel!" If he lags, jerk him up, saying "Heel!" If he tries to go wide, jerk him into you, saying "Heel!" If he crowds against you, bump his head sharply with your knee as you walk, saying "Heel!"

You are likely to have a struggle on your hands. But even if it seems "mean," don't give in when he balks or tugs. Ease up on the tension when the dog is in about the place you want him. The slip-chain collar applies pressure evenly when the dog pulls against it, acting on the big muscles and cords on the side of the neck and in effect throttling him down. When you tug the leash, jerk it quickly and hard. A prolonged steady pull will panic the dog, causing him either to fight more or to lie down and refuse to budge. The slip-chain collar achieves control, but is less likely to injure a dog than the regular leather collar, which applies pressure only to the soft, vulnerable underside of the neck when the dog resists.

A pup must be jerked up to, back to or into the position in which you want him, which ideally is with his shoulder approximately at your knee. To get him into that position you don't have to be brutal, but you must be firm. Jerk him over and say, "Heel!" When he's in the right position, talk nice to him and tell him how well he's doing. Some dogs "get it" the first lesson, others only after a week or two, but eventually, he'll learn that when commanded to "Heel," he can walk in comfort on the leash if he keeps that position. Some dogs will walk along happily, tails up and wagging. Others never do look on it as anything but punishment, and their lowered tails and general attitude reflect this outlook all their lives.

Keep on using plenty of "All Right" release breaks. When the pup has walked along passably for twenty to fifty yards, unsnap the leash, say "All Right," and encourage him to cavort and play. Play with him and reassure him. When his dauber's up again, put the leash back on and repeat the heeling lesson.

Once he's learned to walk in proper position on leash, start off as usual and then, as he is moving along properly, unobtrusively unsnap the leash. As long as he holds position talk to him encouragingly. But if he breaks or lags, sharply command him to "Heel!" If he does, resume the praise and then quickly release him with an "All Right." If he bolts or lags, snap the leash back on and remind him sharply what "Heel" means. Then when he's at it again, try walking him free. Any time he backslides return to the leash and collar, which is the only way you can enforce the heel command. Later, if he gets careless you can plink him with a marble from a slingshot to remind him.

### KENNEL

This command means "Get In There!" and if saying that comes more naturally to you, use it. Just so that the dog understands that without fail, he should jump into the boat, the car, his dog house or kennel crate, or enter anything you point at and say "Kennel!" It's a simple thing to teach. But it's surprising how many people are impressed by a dog who does this with alacrity.

Each time you put your puppy back in his kennel (and you'll have to put him there, for he won't go voluntarily) hold him with one hand, point with the other, snap out "Kennel!" and then "scruff-of-the-neck and seat-of-the-pants him" into the kennel. Since you should be taking him out and putting him back into his confinement area several times a day, this is hardly formal training. If he's kept in the house, do the same thing at the door each time.

On a more formal basis, open the car door or his travel crate door, lead him up to it, point and say, "Kennel!" Assist him in. Praise him. Call him out. Repeat. You may even have to toss him in, once in a while. But soon, when you point and say "Kennel!" he'll jump or run in. One lesson like this will get you well started. As you keep at it and he starts anticipating you and entering before you tell him, make him sit and wait before ordering him to "Kennel!"

The first auto ride! These two Labrador puppies might be just a trifle apprehensive.

## HUNT 'EM OUT

This command is self-explanatory; it's used to start a dog working busily in cover which you have reason to believe contains game, and to encourage a dog who's already working to accelerate his efforts to produce.

As a man who's hunting with a retriever, you'll want the dog to work before the gun and produce birds as well as pick them up after they're shot. Given the chance and encouraged to do so, most retrievers take to this readily. Even the reluctant ones can learn to make something of an effort on command. So while the phrase "Hunt 'em out" won't be found in a field-trial dog's lexicon, it is useful for encouraging an eagerly questing dog, or ordering a reluctant one to work.

The "older puppy," about six months of age, is ready to learn "Hunt 'em out" when he has indicated to you that he can use his nose, such as by winding a dummy he didn't mark too well in deep grass. Some pups not only have "good noses" but seem born with an instinct to know how to use them. Others may actually have a good nose, catching scent readily, but very slowly (and sometimes never) learning how to *locate* the object giving off the scent.

Hide a birdwing-wrapped dummy in grass or other cover. Or sprinkle a few drops of the commercially manufactured duck or pheasant scents on a dummy, or use a freshly killed pigeon or recently-shot game bird if your dog has handled birds. Whatever you use, drop it into cover without the dog seeing it. Then bring him in, at heel, headed into the wind, to maybe five or ten yards from where the object is hidden. Release him with "All Right" and follow him with "Hunt 'em out, Rip! Hunt 'em out!" in excited and encouraging tones, and wave your hand indicating the cover ahead. Guide him toward the bird until he winds it and picks it up.

Then run away from him, clapping and calling, telling him to fetch and tell him what a good dog he is when he does the job.

Work on this as you take the pup for walks until you can call him over to you from whatever he is doing and cast him out, and he'll work busily, quartering the ground until he finds birds within twenty or thirty yards from where he was cast. At first you'll practically have to lead him to the object to be retrieved and point it out, but gradually he'll go out by himself, use his nose and keep reaching. Always head him into the wind and give him every possible chance.

There, that wasn't so bad, was it? And all the while you thought dog training was a dull, repetitous routine, like learning the multiplication tables! Well, a lot of good dogs have been trained that way—but it was work for both dog and trainer. You're not earning your living doing this. It's a hobby, so enjoy it! If a dog is a slow learner, the by-rote, one-step-at-a-time method may have to be resorted to. But there's no point in laboriously setting one training "block" on top of another, step by step, when you can lay up a whole stack or leap up the steps three-at-a-time.

Your retriever is now ready to take hunting. No, I haven't forgotten the gun. But it's an important enough item to be dealt with separately. Then you won't ever have to try to "cure" gunshyness. It won't happen, if your dog and the gun are properly introduced.

Just because you now know how much and how easily a young pup can learn, don't get carried away by this training bit and forget that "all work and no play can make Rip a dull tool." While I honestly doubt that most of you will overdo it, the over-zealous must remember that even though you were "play-training" the pup, a certain amount of coercion was used and you were serious about this "play." That prize of yours is still a puppy and he has to be allowed to be a puppy. Give him time to play, by himself and according to his whims. Let the kids romp with him. You rough-house with him and pet him and talk to him. Let him snuffle around on his own when you have him out. Take him with you wherever and whenever you can. It will take some added effort; but it will pay off in the form of a well-adjusted companion dog. A field-trial dog is a hunting machine, pure and simple. A hunting dog should also be 'a family dog and companion.

From three months on, take him for hikes and walks in the woods. You won't overtire him. His growing muscles need the exercise he'd get romping with his litter mates. Let him piddle and puddle about on his own on leisurely strolls, so that the great out-of-doors, fences, domestic animals and the strange sights and sounds of his future "workshop" will be familiar to him when the hunting season rolls around.

"But, but, but," a few of you are going to say "I have a retriever pup of good breeeding and he cost plenty. But he isn't doing the retrieving as easy and naturally as you said he would."

True, friend, true. This book isn't written on the basis of having trained one puppy who happened to be good. Your problems have also been my problems at one time or another.

Your pup does one of four things. He runs away from you with the dummy; he plays with it or chews it instead of coming toward you; he won't pick it up; or he drops it before he gets to you. The *real* problems, as they come up with older dogs, will be dealt with separately. Meantime, here's what to do to prevent these puppy antics from becoming full-fledged trouble.

## PUP RUNS OFF WITH DUMMY

Don't chase him. That's the game he wants to play. You go in the opposite direction, calling and clapping. Even duck around the corner, so he'll come looking for you. He really isn't as cocky as he acts. You're his buddy, and he's a little lost without you. If he brings the dummy with him, wonderful. Praise him. If not, go pick it up. Start over, teasing and rolling it out front. He'll bring it near you sometime, even accidentally. Then praise. If he runs off (remember we're inside, the pup is small, so he can't go far) move away, call and hide on him. Keep at it. This isn't nearly as serious as:

## PUP WON'T PICK UP DUMMY

This calls for running a slight risk of developing hard mouth. Tease more with the dummy, encouraging him to grab, even shake. A glove or sock is better than a dummy here. When his "blood is up" slide it out for him. He'll pounce on it, and may even bring it to you as the source of all this devilment. If he doesn't, move away and call him. It's a lot of teasing and foolish play and involves some risk. But very

often in training a pup or dog, you risk possible establishment of a
future bad habit in an effort to accomplish something or solve an
immediate problem. There's nothing cut-and-dried about dog training.

As a last resort, when the pup is six to eight months old, if he still
is not picking up and carrying naturally, you may have to resort to
formal "forced-retrieving" training. This method will be outlined in
the section dealing with pointing dogs, since such force-training frequently must be resorted to for these dogs. In the case of retrievers,
quite frankly, I don't think it's worth bothering with one who has to
be taught by punishment, pain or rote to do what his heritage says
should come naturally, namely picking up and carrying.

### PUP MAULS OR CHEWS DUMMY INSTEAD OF BRINGING IT

When the pup lies down with the dummy or glove and starts abusing
it, call him a couple of times and move away from him, clapping.

If he won't respond, quickly walk up to him, say "No, bad dog!"
or "Cut it out, you little s.o.b.!" depending on your mood. Then take
the dummy from him briskly, and swat him lightly on the rear. Having
made him aware of your disapproval, move back away from him,
squat down and call him to you. Make up with him, get him interested
in the dummy, and try sliding or tossing it out again. Repeat as often
as necessary.

With this antic and the one in which the pup runs away from you,
you may also try a shortcut if your patience wears thin. Attach a light
cord to the pup's collar, once he's become accustomed to it. When he
picks up the dummy, gently but firmly reel him in as you tell him to
fetch, take the dummy from him gently and praise him highly. Repeat
until he comes of his own accord. This is the nearest thing to a "sure
cure" for those ills. I usually take a little more time playing and coaxing,
simply because I get a kick out of messing with pups and I like happy
as well as reliable workers.

### PUP DROPS DUMMY AND LEAVES IT WHEN RETURNING

This is most often caused by anxious handlers moving toward the pup
(a threat) or trying to grab the dummy before the pup gets to his
handler. This action can also result in the pup running away with the
dummy. Sometimes the object the pup is asked to carry is too large.
That's why the glove and sock were suggested to start with.

Always move away from your pup as he comes in, even to the extent
of taking the dummy on the run as he catches up with you and goes

past. This isn't too serious, just yet. If you can't coax the pup out of this, we'll explain, in an up-coming section on problems with older dogs, how to deal with this so that your dog will make a complete and clean delivery.

Your pup is now five months, eight months or maybe a year old or more, and he has his basics behind him. You want to get hunting. So, what's holding you back? Good man! That little gem of yours hasn't been shot over yet. You don't want him to be gunshy. He won't be, if you turn the page and start his introduction to the gun.

# 8

## Gunshot Training

The epitome of worthlessness is a gunshy hunting dog.

Yes, a gunshy dog *is* born now and then. But this "sensitive," "nervous," "spooky," or whatever term someone may use to describe a "kook" he's trying to foist off on someone else, *isn't* really a problem—because he isn't worth working with in the first place! Everything "bugs" the shy dog, and his total lack of temperament is obvious to anyone with a modicum of familiarity with animals. Any loud noise "upsets" him enough to cause cringing, slinking, snapping or urinating.

Don't ever get a shy pup just because you feel sorry for him. And if you are unfortunate enough to already own one of these psycho's, get rid of it, preferably by having it humanely put down so there's no risk of its perpetuating its kind. Some mild cases are still trainable, but hardly worth the time and effort, since it's slow, slow, slow; and just when you've made headway, something crops up that spooks this kind of dog all over again.

Even if it's not born in a dog, gunshyness can be made, and in fact, it's often an acquired trait, mostly manmade. Once it's established, you'll have the devil's own time curing it. So it follows that the most sensible thing to do is prevent it. This is easy to do.

You already have a good start if you've been banging feed pans, slamming doors, clapping your hands and generally making loud noises around a puppy. He's become accustomed to noise. It's part of life and doesn't hurt him. The food-pan noise is connected with something pleasant. That's just how you're going to prevent gunshyness, associating something that's fun for the dog with gunfire. I'm not talking about messing around shooting off cap pistols every time you feed the dog.

There are bold pups and cautious pups. You should know what your own pup is by the time you're ready to introduce him to guns and gunfire. If he greets every new experience like a long lost litter mate, you'll be able to shortcut. If he's hesitant until assured everything is okay, take it step by step.

The Irish Water Spaniel pictured in some of this book's illustrations is a good case in point. His introduction to gunfire was simple. From his car crate in the back of the station wagon he watched me testing a device that uses blank cartridges to propel a retrieving dummy. He had been exposed to noises since I got him at seven weeks of age, and had been "play-trained" to retrieve. After he'd watched a couple of the older dogs go out and fetch the shot-propelled dummy, I took him out and let him gambol around. He was six months old. When he was a little way off I spoke his name to attract his attention and shot off the device. He saw the dummy in the air, galloped out, picked it up and came back as though he'd been doing it for months.

It can be that easy. But don't count on it. Instead, follow this procedure. It is applicable to both spaniels and retrievers, and to a large extent can be used with the Continental pointing breeds. (It's not generally suitable for Pointers and setters, so we'll take them up separately.)

My pups are usually fired over for the first time at an age of from five to seven months. By that time they are retrieving, very often have been taken along hunting, and think this is about the greatest game in the world. Yours should too.

An assistant, son, daughter, wife or friend, armed with a handgun and .22 blanks, should be stationed about thirty yards from you. Position your pup at your side, ready to retrieve, and key him up by talking to him encouragingly.

At your nod the assistant shoots, aiming away from the dog, and tosses the dummy high in the air. Make the retrieve an easy one, not too far and in plain sight. The shot will get your pup's attention and he'll see what should be a familiar sight—a dummy in the air. That's when

Dave Duffey prepares to fire a useful but relatively expensive training device which throws a fetching dummy with a blank charge, as an Irish Water Spaniel sits and waits.

Duffey shoots the dummy, while cautioning the eight-month-old pup to wait.

The pup has gone out, and now comes trotting back with the dummy, which had been shot out about sixty yards. This device helps the dog to associate gunfire with an object to retrieve, and also saves the arm of the trainer!

The puppy makes a clean delivery to Duffey.

you say, "Rip, Fetch!" If he's half the pup we think he is, he'll be on his way. Praise him when he completes the retrieve.

All this is is another "fun" lesson in retrieving, with the added noise of a gunshot. Give him half a dozen retrieves, each with a gunshot. You may be able to move your assistant in closer before you finish the day's five or six retrieves. If the dog seems a bit bothered by the shooting, move the assistant out and have the dummy tossed toward the dog. The idea is that the dog likes to retrieve, it's fun and he's praised for it. Through association he'll quickly learn to look for something to fetch whenever he hears gunfire.

Over a period of several days, work your assistant in closer, and eventually you can do the shooting yourself, pointing the gun in the air. It shouldn't be necessary to mention this, but—*never* pop even a .22 next to a pup's head. If a hunting partner of yours has ever "touched one off" where muzzle blast assaulted your ears, you know why.

After the pup's got the .22 down pat, move up to a shotgun. Almost always a 12-gauge is okay if your assistant is far enough off, fifty yards or so to start, and aims away from you and the dog. The steps are the same, with the assistant gradually working closer until finally you are handling the gun and doing the shooting.

You can do this in a couple of days or spread it out over weeks and months, depending upon your diligence and your pup's precociousness. In any event, get it behind you before the hunting season starts. You'll want to be able to shoot at the first bird your pup puts up, for this is important, indicating that this is what you want him to do. In the last analysis, killing birds over a dog is what really "makes him," with or without proper yard training. And he'll quickly learn that a gun makes for a catchable rather than an unobtainable bird.

As an added safeguard, sometime before the hunting season opens get hold of some barn pigeons. Have a friend toss them into flight and have another, who's a good shot, kill them, while you send your dog out to fetch when they drop.

After the pup has done this satisfactorily, dizzy a pigeon, plant it in cover, work your pup toward it and tell him to "Hunt 'em out!" Maybe you dizzied it too much. He catches it. Fine. You're going to expect him to catch cripples, and a spaniel or retriever flushes because he's trying to catch. It's good training. When things go right and the bird gets into the air shoot it, or have a companion who's a good shot down it, being careful that your wild, chasing pup isn't close enough to be sprinkled with shot. If you miss and the pup chases, let him go. He's young and shouldn't be restrained—yet. In many states, birds from game farms, like chukar and pheasant, are allowed under permit

Pigeons are cheap, and readily available for use in training all breeds of dogs. Here an American Water Spaniel holds one that was shot for him to retrieve.

for dog-training; these are superior to pigeons, except that they cost a lot more and aren't as easy to obtain.

Give your pup all the experience you can on birds before the hunting season. You then eliminate any possibility that a cackling rooster or a drumming partridge, something really new to him, will startle him. If this surprise is backed up by a loud gunshot, it may upset his composure enough to make you back-track on his training until he regains confidence. Until he's had a year of hunting behind him, I wouldn't put him in a blind full of hunters either. A cannonade of shooting when he can't see, smell or hear game isn't going to make much sense to him, and could cause grief for both of you.

Don't let some friend suggest that "we take your pup out and shoot over him a few times to find out if he's gunshy." With friends like that, who needs enemies? You should be sure he isn't gunshy, thanks to yard-training, before you start banging away in the field.

Nor should you let someone talk you into taking your dog to a trap or skeet range, "just to get him used to shooting." One of two things will happen. A placid dog will come to ignore gunfire. A high-strung one will be driven out of his mind by the senseless (to him) blasting. Neither reaction is desirable in a gun dog.

Do the job right and your retriever or spaniel will jump with joy and wiggle in anticipation when you pull your shotgun out of the case, look up alertly when the action snicks open and the shells are shoved in. He'll try to spot a bird in the air when the gun goes off, or if he fails to mark the fall, he'll quest about busily until he finds it, firm in his belief that "there's just gotta be a bird down out here."

# 9

## Advanced Retrieving

### WATER RETRIEVES

In addition to gunfire and birds, there are lots of other things a retriever (or spaniel) must learn about. A very important one is water.

Every dog, at one time or another, is going to be asked to fetch a downed bird out of the water—retrievers certainly, spaniels often, Continental pointing breeds sometimes, and even Pointers and setters upon occasion.

Pups can be introduced to water at an early age during the warm summer months. Youngsters from eight weeks on can be induced to splash around in the shallows. If your pup was whelped at the wrong time for this, wait till spring comes and a day is hot, the marshes wet and the fields puddled, and then put on your hip boots and do some puddling around, taking your dog with you. He'll follow you through the shallows, get used to water and enjoy it as long as he doesn't get chilled; and running and moving about on a sunny day, he won't.

For pups whelped in winter or spring, wait until the water is warm,

anywhere from mid-June on, depending upon your location. Don't pick
a raw spring day right after the ice has gone. As usual in dog training,
this is a matter of common sense and getting the pup accustomed to
something through playing. Once he's found that romping in the water
is fun, occasional unpleasant experiences he may undergo won't dampen
his enthusiasm.

The next step is to pick a calm, quiet lake or pothole where both
you and the pup can wade. There is little excuse for a water-shy retriever or spaniel; perhaps they don't all express the same desire and
fondness for water, but most take to the water so naturally that a man
almost has to work at it to spoil them. In contrast, some of the pointing
dogs are almost like cats in their avoidance of water, although they
too can be introduced to it in the manner I'm outlining here.

However, it's up to you to decide whether it's worth the bother to
water-train a pointer or setter. But you *should* do it with one of the Continental pointing breeds, and must do it with a retriever or spaniel.

Be alone with your pup or only take along one or two members of
the family who know what you're doing. Don't go to a beach with lots of
people and excitement. Also take an older, experienced water dog along
if you can—he may entice the pup into the water. On a warm day,
however, almost any dog or pup will wade out into the shallows to
lap or loll in the water. In your swim-trunks or waders, you wade too.

Encourage the pup to follow you, if he isn't already frolicking a bit
in the water. Maybe he'll stand on shore and bark. Just keep coaxing.
You may even have to pick him up, cuddle and pet him, set him
down gently in the water and let him scamper to shore, barely getting
his legs wet. When he's in the water with you, move about slowly,
sweet-talking him. You may even resort to tossing bits of bread or
meat out in front of his nose to encourage him to go out farther, if he
seems reluctant to follow you.

Eventually he'll get out over his depth and be swimming before he
knows it. He'll swim naturally, maybe with some splashing with the
forepaws. He'll probably turn and head for shore, feeling for footing.
Let him. Let him shake off and play on the shore for a time. Then
start him playing in the water all over. After several of these coaxing,
playing sessions he'll probably be quite bold. If not, keep at the playing.

You may be lucky enough to have some crazy, bold pup who will
fall in or jump in himself, or try some scary antic that would shake
up a less confident pup. Count your blessings! But don't give up on the
slower, cautious pup. He can be coaxed in, too. If you have a litter of
puppies and all are taken to water at the same time, the boldness of a
few, the playing and the rivalry, will probably get most of the rest of
them into the water.

## NEVER THROW A PUP IN

Just go slow and easy. Don't expect and don't encourage your pup to jump off a bank, dock or out of a boat. Above all, *don't ever* throw a puppy into the water. For all but the most foolhardy, an unwilling immersion can discourage him not only temporarily but perhaps permanently. Teaching him to jump in only comes after he's well accustomed to water. Some dogs never do take a big leap out into the water, preferring to slide in. There's nothing wrong with this, as long as they go willingly—it's just less spectacular. If your pup is already retrieving fairly well on land before you acquaint him with water, you can often cut out most of this introductory stuff.

## A FETCHING INTRODUCTION

Take the pup's dummy to the shallow, warm-water place you've selected. First have him fetch on land for a time or two, and then flip the dummy just a foot or two out into the water. He'll step out and reach to pick it up and may even pounce on it. Gradually increase the distance until he has to wade to get it. As he gets more confident, keep increasing the distance until it's just beyond his depth, so he'll make a lunge to grab the dummy and his front feet won't reach bottom. Then gradually increase the distance until he has to swim a few feet to the dummy before turning and coming back.

As a rule, you can't do this all in one day. Take it easy, four or five fetches a day being enough. You don't want him to quit because you threw it too far or too often. Refusals can become a habit, and once instilled they're hard to break. You want success. To make sure of achieving it, a pup must wade before he can swim. This is not a training exercise to see how far he'll swim or how well he'll mark a fall. It's part of water introduction. It is a doubling-up of training procedure, but the emphasis is on making him confident in water.

Maybe he is showing more than average willingness and aptitude. Resist the temptation to push him too far. Eventually, you'll have him going out as far as you can throw the dummy, swimming strongly. At that stage, if he should turn to come back without the dummy, you can wade out with him and make him pick it up. But always be sure that when a dummy splats on the water he completes a retrieve.

After he's swimming well and entering the water with a rush, you can get him to jump off a dock or low bank. Tease him with the dummy and get him excited, then drop it into the water just out of reach. Chances are he'll try to get it with one leap. This will get him

"Sit!"—a basic command for a retriever, is performed by *McGurk*, an American Water Spaniel, as part of his training at the hands of his nine-year-old mistress, Deborah Duffey.

At first, the dummy is thrown only a short distance, though later it is thrown as far as you can throw it. *McGurk* obediently waits for it to plunk out into the water.

He's picked up the dummy, and is heading back just as fast as he can. This is fun, and the dog shouldn't be restrained too long until he's really eager to fetch, and knows what the score is.

"Sit, and Hold It!" Sitting to deliver may not be a necessity, but it *is* a nicety in a retriever, and here *McGurk* obeys both commands.

"Good dog, *McGurk!*" Praise is important in training a dog, and nobody praises better than a little girl whose dog has done his lesson right.

Proud? You bet! Though she's too young to shoot the duck herself, she was along to see how her summer training paid off for Dad, when he used her little dog on opening day.

This Springer Spaniel really "lays out" over the water on the way to his retrieve.

in the habit of "hitting the water hard" rather than slipping in. Do this first from something stationary, rather than a boat. The rocking of the boat or striking his legs on the gunwales when he jumps out may spook him.

## BOATS AND MOTORS

Your retriever or spaniel is going to be in some kind of a boat, usually motor-powered, frequently or at least at some time during his life. So the best introduction is to have him around them, letting him jump in and out of a boat or boats as he's doing his training sessions in water. But this can also be done at home, with the boat on land.

Tell him to "Kennel!" and have him jump into the boat. Unless you make him sit and wait, he'll probably jump right out again. Let him do this a few times as he develops confidence. You may have to get into the boat yourself and coax him in, telling him to "Kennel!" Then later you can point and tell him to get in.

With you in the boat, have him sit quietly for a time and talk to him in an encouraging manner, rather than rapping him if he doesn't settle down right away (for the boat rocking may make him apprehen-

"Hey—that water's deep!" A group of Labrador Retriever puppies gets used to a boat and water early in life, at only eight weeks of age.

sive). Pet him, and tell him how good he is as he sits in front of you.

After you've made him sit and talked with him for a while, and he's not dejected or shivering, step out of the boat and wade or walk around it, cautioning him to wait. Then release him with an "All right!" and call him to you. Chances are good that he'll leap out. If he doesn't, coax him out. If you can't coax him out, leave him there and walk off. He won't stay. He'll follow you. He's now started learning how to enter and leave a boat.

For his first ride, get a stable boat, so he can move around a bit with no danger of tipping. (Save the duck skiffs and canoes for later.) Let him get used to the motion and to the boat before you enforce any "sitting quietly" regulations. When he's confident, make him sit and wait. You should row or paddle, and let the motor come later.

To have him jump out of the boat, start in shallow water, where his feet will hit bottom. At first, you get out in the water yourself and call him. Once he's jumping out and coming to you in no more than belly-deep water, have him sit and wait in the boat, then toss a retrieving dummy, close enough the first few times so he'll try to leap on it. Eventually toss it farther. All this calls for repetition, and the speed at which you progress will depend upon the dog's precocity and courage. Finally, moor the boat in swimming water and have him start jumping out from there to retrieve a tossed dummy. When he

How to double up on training: here a dog gets accustomed to a boat (on dry land) and gets some retrieving practice at the same time.

A helper (in this case, professional trainer Orin Benson) can toss the dummy, or the trainer can throw his own. Duffey cautions the young Chesapeake to remain steady until sent.

Calling his dog's name and swinging his arm, Duffey sends the Chesapeake out of the boat and into the water after the dummy.

The dog returns with the dummy, and Duffey will climb into the boat and have the retriever bring the dummy to him and deliver it there.

starts back toward you with it, row the boat back into the shallows, step out and have him deliver to you while you're in the shallow water, praising him highly.

When this has gone well, climb back into the boat and get him to jump from the shallow water into the boat and deliver the dummy to you there. At first maybe you'll have to beach the boat before you coax him into it. The idea is to have him deliver to you no matter where you may be. Don't do this in deep water until he has become an experienced retriever.

When he likes swimming, and knows the boat is a safe resting place that he likes to ride in and enjoys working from, sit him on shore, row out a way and call him to you. He'll want to come and should be accustomed to the boat from previous training. When he comes up alongside, help him in. He'll try to hook his forelegs over the gunwhale. Place your hand behind his head where it joins the neck, pull and he'll brace and come up out of the deep water into the boat. Whether you want him to deliver a dummy or duck while he's alongside or after he's in the boat is your choice. But since he may clamp down hard as he struggles to get in, delivery alongside is the wisest choice.

The outboard motor means a new noise, and vibration. So get out into deep water, where he won't be tempted to jump back onto the dock or shore if he decides to desert, and then start the motor and take him for a ride. Don't be too harsh if he's a bit restless at first. Speak calmly and reassure him and he'll find out it's okay. Take him as frequently as possible. Most dogs love it and the least he'll do is accept it as a way of life. After he's confident and relaxed, enforce "sit" and "wait" commands so he won't ram around.

## DECOYS

A lot of waterfowl hunters don't use decoys. So if you're a jump shooter, or a "scratch 'em down when they come over the pass" advocate, you can skip this. However, at one time or another your dog is probably going to encounter decoys, and getting him to ignore them in favor of the real thing is so simple that it's worth doing, if only to avoid your being embarrassed if he should spook when asked to work through blocks, or even worse, make a spectacular retrieve of an imitation duck!

Scatter some blocks out on your lawn. Walk the pup through them at heel. If he shows the slightest interest in them, tell him "No!" and swat him across the flank. When he's convinced these fakes hold no charm for him, toss a dummy beyond them and send him through them to fetch. Then toss it off to the sides, and finally right among

Retrievers can be trained to ignore decoys if at first you place the decoys on land, and have the dog run through them. This Chesapeake is going out to retrieve a shackled duck.

them. He'll pick up what he's been praised for and ignore the things that earned him a cuff.

Then when you're working him in water, take the decoys along and throw a few out, working him among and through them. After only a couple of lessons he'll no more think of picking one up than he'd plan on towing the boat home.

## DUMMIES AND REAL BIRDS

Throughout these training suggestions we've talked about "dummies" —the kapok-filled, canvas-covered or plastic boat fenders that a spaniel or retriever learns his fetching on. You should understand, however, that once the rudiments of retrieving have been mastered and your pup knows what feathers are, you can use shot or shackled game-farm birds, domestic mallards, or pigeons, instead of a steady diet of dummies, and you should.

Here's how a retriever can learn hunting by chasing down a wing-clipped duck. A young Golden Retriever gets a close look at the quarry, a pen-raised mallard.

Mr. Mallard is put down in the cover to hide, before the dog is released to track him do

The young Golden hunts and drives the duck out into the open, and closes
in to make the retrieve.

ιn eager dog, he scoops up the mallard on the run and heads back to the ·ainer. A properly started retriever won't harm even a live, struggling duck.

The point is, however, that a retriever or spaniel can be made ready for the hunting field at a considerable saving in money, time and effort through the use of dummies. They are also always available when a man has just a few minutes, and wants to either brush his dog up on some particular phase or just give him a bit of work. Should you ever find your dog going stale in his retrieving work, switch to shackled birds. They'll perk him up.

## TRACKING AND CATCHING "CRIPS"

Of great value in the hunting field is the dog who recovers crippled birds which don't stay where they dropped. Some pre-season work on this can go a long way toward your being able to smile proudly and accept your friends' congratulations, after your dog has collected a "runner" hundreds of yards from where he dropped, or emerged from a quest out into the marsh with a duck that no one in your party shot.

Start with a wing-clipped barn pigeon. Throw it out on the lawn or into a mowed field where the dog can see it. Send him for it. It's really no challenge, but it'll get him used to running down moving game and returning it to you intact. If your dog is soft-mouthed (and most retrievers are when introduced to game as we have done in our preliminary lessons), you'll be able to use one pigeon dozens of times. But don't get worried if a few die. Some expire from shock or fright, others because the dog happens to grab them just right—or just wrong from the pigeon's point of view. Unless your dog is actually crunching them, he isn't hard-mouthed.

Then progress to heavier cover. The dog will have to use his nose more. From there, go to a shackled or wing-clipped domestic mallard. Toss it in a small marshy spot or in a field with high cover and send your dog for it. The duck can lead him a merry chase. If you pick too big an area, it might even escape. So until your pup has done pretty well, don't release just willy-nilly. Make sure his chances of success are good the first few times and make it tough later on.

Finally, try it in water, a pothole or small creek, where the duck will head for the marsh or shore rather than staying in open water. A dog can catch a "cripple" in a marsh, but in open water the duck

ιppy with his work, the Golden isn't too anxious to release his game, and ffey moves his hand under the lower jaw and pinches the lip against the teeth in order to effect a release.

may be able to elude the pup at least long enough to discourage him and make him quit. Don't let that happen, even if you have to go out and catch the duck yourself and hold it for the pup.

Ducks are almost indestructible if the dog is any kind of a retriever. A brace of ducks, alternated so they don't soak up too much, will last you for as long as you want to train. They can be used in all aspects of the retriever's training whenever convenient, and should be used at least every now and then to spice things up and keep the dog sharp. Ducks will last longer if their wings are taped to their bodies when they are used in water work, or they can be encased in a restraining "sweater" that can either be purchased commercially or made from an old sweat sock. You may want to put a rubber band around a duck's bill. They get sassy when they find out they aren't going to get hurt, and will grab a dog's ear or lip. This will frighten a soft pup, and sometimes fire up a tough one so he'll bite back—both undesirable happenings.

You now have a fair-to-middlin' trained huntin' dog ready to go, but there are three more things you are going to want to work on. They're going to make a lot of your friends either shake their heads in disbelief, or lay down their money for a dog of their own.

## HUNTING IN GUN RANGE

As an upland hunter as well as a waterfowler you're figuring on your Lab, Golden, Ches or Irish working out in front of you to flush birds as well as to fetch what you shoot. You're hoping he'll stay within gun range. Otherwise, you'll do a lot of chasing and cussing but very little primer popping. You don't have to hope. You can do it. Most retrievers, given a chance and encouragement, will hunt before the gun and work sensibly close.

Now I have to ask a favor. I don't want to write the same thing twice, and since this business of training a dog to hunt within gun range is primarily applicable to spaniels, I'll have to ask you to turn to the spaniel section. All the advice about spaniels in this regard also applies to retrievers. By the same token, we're going to ask the spaniel trainers to refer to the retriever section to learn about fetching, introduction to water, etc. Having taken that in, let's proceed with:

## MULTIPLE MARKED RETRIEVERS, AND STEADINESS

A dog can be trained to remember where two or three birds fell that were killed in one volley of shots, and collect them one-at-a-time at your command. However, it stands to reason that unless he is steady (stays put wherever stationed until sent to retrieve) he's going to miss something. It's doubtful that he'll see the second or third bird fall if he's already started after the first. And even if he does, he's likely to get confused when the splat of a falling duck in the water distracts him from his original course.

So keep working on your "Wait!" (or "Stay," or "Whoa," or "Steady" or whatever you say) without let-up, until you are positive—well, pretty sure, anyhow—that your dog won't leap out of the boat or blind or off a muskrat house just because a shot is fired. It'll save a lot of wasted effort, and some unneeded moisture and discomfort if your dog doesn't take off every time you shoot and miss—which I'm assuming you do at least as frequently as I do.

As outlined earlier, steadiness is taught by having the dog wait at your side during retrieving lessons until you send him. But you can keep this foremost in your dog's mind every time you have him with you by asking him to "Sit and Wait!" while you walk off, or by leaving him or stationing him somewhere while you go about something else.

Only through experience will a hunting retriever, like this Labrador, learn to look in the direction in which the gun is pointing in order to quickly mark a falling duck.

Tempt him to go at times before you give the "All right!" release, but scold him and put him back to stay for a while, if and when he succumbs.

*Do not,* however, enforce this steadiness test in conjunction with retrieving lessons until your pup is a real nut on retrieving, who will boil out there for long single retrieves seventy-five to a hundred yards away. You can't throw a dummy or dead bird that far? Neither can I. You need a helper to stand that distance away, shoot a gun and throw. When the dog has demonstrated his desire and fondness for fetching, restrain him gently but firmly at first, but let him go while the dummy's still in the air. Then just keep holding him a bit longer, until he'll stay of his own accord until sent.

When he's sitting steady enough so that, while he may jitter and shift, he can be talked into staying until sent, he's ready to start marking more than one dummy. If he breaks at this stage you can crack down and make him stay, resting assured that he won't think you're trying to discourage his fetching. The time for this is determined by the pup's stage in training, not by his age.

Even so, I certainly would not require more than a semblance of steadiness (and therefore wouldn't start multiple retrieves) before the age of six to eight months, and then only with a precocious pup. For if you are doing "doubles" before this time with an average pup, either your dog is not solidly grounded in his basics, or you've been over-zealous and will burn the pup out before he's ready.

## FETCHING A PAIR

When you first start multiple retrieves they should not be long (certainly no farther than you can throw the dummy from your position alongside the dog, and preferably shorter, for an opener) and the dummies should be tossed where the dog can easily spot them. Make sure he sees them both fall, and attract his attention to the second dummy you toss if he's got his eyes glued on the first. Send him as soon as the second dummy hits the ground.

To send him, say "Rip! Fetch!"—or just "Rip!" if he goes on name alone, which is a good procedure if you are working more than one dog, or have field-trial aspirations. Swing your arm as if you were aiming for a ten-strike in the direction of the second dummy, which he should get first. If he's done well on singles this won't be any problem. But the other dummy is a toughie; be prepared.

A pup with a good memory will probably start toward the other dummy as he comes back with the first one he's picked up. *This is good.*

But don't let him do it. "Beep, Beep, Beep" him on the whistle and call him to you, even running out to intercept him if necessary.

Then sit him at your side, aiming him generally in the direction of the unretrieved dummy. (They should be widely spread when thrown, to discourage his crossing or switching on the way in or out, and to accustom him to heading in a different direction for his second retrieve.)

Send him as quickly as possible, with the same bowling-ball sweep of your arm, in the direction of the second dummy. He may remember it or, if it's close enough and in the open, see it and go to it. Wonderful! There are going to be times in the future when he forgets, but you have a head start.

But maybe he'll start, and then whip around and look at you, puzzled. He's forgotten. Or he may even head in the wrong direction. Don't fret. Most pups do this at first. Walk out toward the dummy with him, gesticulating (underarm sweep) and encouraging him to "Fetch!" When he does locate it and pick it up, trot back to your original position, with him running back with you and toting the dummy. Take it from him there. Praise him and keep repeating the exercise. It won't be long (unless he's hopelessly stupid) before he'll start on faith alone even if he doesn't recall the second "bird," but then see the dummy and go to it. And pretty soon, after completing the first delivery, he'll be sitting looking off in the direction of the second one, remembering.

Gradually increase the distance the dummies are thrown until they're out far enough for you to need helpers to toss them. You should also start throwing them in cover, so the dog will have to start "marking the area of the fall," going to it and using his nose until he recovers the "bird."

For triples the procedure is the same, except that you use three dummies or birds. Four or five? This is pointless. I have yet to see a dog I thought capable of remembering more than three falls, and going beyond that can only lead to confusion and grief.

Although you have used the "underarm pitch" hand signal to send your dog on singles, I presume, it was really only a sign to go out there and get what he knew was there. So now in the doubles training, you've taken the first step in teaching your retriever his second hand signal. (The first, you'll recall, was the upraised arm in conjunction with "Sit!" and one sharp whistle blast.)

## GIVING AND TAKING A LINE

That "bowler's sweep" of the arm, which you've just been using to send your dog on his way to a marked retrieve will also be used to "give him a line"—to guide him in the completion of a "blind retrieve," which occurs when the dog either did not see the bird fall, or obviously forgot about it; but nevertheless recovers it by responding to whistle and hand signals.

Once a retriever learns to "take a line" he can be taught with diligent training to make spectacular casts, going straight as a string for up to two hundred yards, until he scents a bird or is stopped by his handler's whistle and redirected.

As a practical matter, a hunting dog seldom does this. For one thing, a retriever that learns to hunt before the gun has learned to quarter or "punch out" to likely looking spots. It's against his nature and habit to "line out."

Besides, few hunters are calm enough, once they have a bird down, to refrain from offering assistance. Hunters will usually walk to the area of a difficult unmarked or unremembered fall, or pole over in a boat, and then gesture to the dog and tell him to "Hunt 'em out!" depending upon the dog to bustle about diligently until he hits scent. This is a generally satisfactory method, for most game is recovered, and you've already trained your dog for this.

But though the long line is thus primarily a field-trial performance, it is useful in instances when it's impossible for a man to get to the area of the fall, and it's certainly a stunt that will make any man justifiably proud of his dog and his training ability. Besides, every good hunting dog should be taught to make the straight-line cast of twenty-five to fifty yards which may be necessary to put him in the area of the fall. So you can teach it this way:

Place a dummy in plain sight, twenty-five to fifty yards from you and the dog. Let him see it placed. Send him from the retrieving position with the usual command and underarm sweep. He'll go get it. Keep lengthening the distance. Then let him see you drop it in cover. (You can do this alone, stationing the dog, going out and dropping the dummy, returning to the dog and then sending him. It's good steadying practice, too.) Send the same way. When he masters this, don't let him see you hide the dummy. Station him where he can't see you (behind a building or car, again good steadying practice). Don't hide the dummy too far away at first, but keep increasing the distance, so he'll keep reaching out until he stumbles on it or scents it.

If you ask for more than fifty-yard lines, or if the dog isn't doing too well on the shorter stuff, you can help to keep him undeviatingly on his course by sending him down a narrow, snowplowed road, a mowed strip in a field, or any other path. He'll naturally follow the "course of least resistance," and the habit of lining straight out is instilled. Ideally, he should continue on line until stopped on command or until he hits bird or dummy scent. So always put the "bird" on the side of the path that will give him the benefit of the wind as he goes by it. He'll hook into it when he hits the scent.

This calls for a lot of repetitious work, but if you'll mix it up in your training sessions with a variety of marked retrieves and other training procedures, it will be less tedious for both you and the dog. When doing marked retrieves, by the way, don't have your dummies tossed at the same angles or distance all the time. You're training a hunting dog, and birds can fall at some odd angles and into strange places. Every now and then, shoot and throw a dummy out while your dog is coming in with another, but don't let him switch, and only send him back for it after he's completed his first retrieve. Do this in the water too, finally dropping one right in front of him as he's coming into the shallows. If he tries to switch, splash out there saying "No!" repeatedly, and dissuade him. This will prevent his swimming around madly if you happen to get a crack at some ducks overhead, while he's out fetching some that were knocked down earlier.

When you've reached this stage of the game, your dog should be reliably stopping to sit on whistle blast, upraised arm or verbal command to halt. (This is especially important if he's being worked in front of you as a spaniel; again, refer to spaniel training section.) If you're approaching this sensibly and training thoroughly, your dog should be this far advanced only after he's had a season or two of hunting under his collar. (I don't believe in instilling mechanical responses in a dog until he's imbued with a desire to hunt. If he lacks this desire, you're wasting a lot of valuable time making him mechanically perfect, since a half-trained dog with the proper enthusiasm for his job will get you more birds.)

After the dog has learned to "line out" on land he should also do it in water, but you'll have to give him some work along these lines, too. This will then allow you to put him across a ditch, river, pothole or other obstacle and into a cover clump on the other side where a bird may have come down. Start off in relatively shallow water, so that you can walk the dog out to the dummy if he balks or refuses to go all the way.

## *"GET OVER," AND "GET BACK"*

The finishing touches in teaching a dog to handle involve his going to the right, left, or straight back on your hand signal, when he's some distance from you. Whether you get a casual or "sometime" response or a precise one depends entirely upon the time and effort you want to put into this phase.

Response to these hand signals is not only valuable in directing a dog to the area where an unmarked bird fell should he deviate from his original line, pass it upwind, or not get out far enough, but it also helps to direct him to a piece of cover you may want worked out.

The formal way to teach this, which results in precise performance, is to let the dog see a dummy some twenty-five to fifty yards to his left, right or straight behind him, as he sits facing you. Position the dog, and then step back about ten yards from him at first, keeping him in a sitting position with upraised hand.

To encourage him to pivot and go straight back to a dummy behind him, make a decisive jump forward, sweep down and forward with your arm, snapping out his name and telling him to "Get Back!"

To get him to go in either direction, leap to the side and sweep down hard with the left or right arm, depending upon which way you want him to go, pointing dramatically in that direction and shouting, "Get Over!" If he goes in the wrong direction, hit him with the whistle and redirect him.

If he hesitates on the "Get Back!" keep moving toward him, repeating "Get Back!" and forcing him out toward the dummy.

If he hesitates on the "Get Over!", keep hopping sideways and waving and pointing in the direction you want him to go, repeating "Get Over!" Since the dummy should be in plain sight and not too far, you won't need as much of this strenuous urging as when you later advance to hiding it.

Keep at this until your dog starts to anticipate your signals by looking in the direction of the dummy, or edging that way and bounding out there at your first gesture. Naturally you always have him deliver to you, and you praise when he does right.

Then hide the dummy. Start all over again with the signals. If you've implanted the routine well, he'll start in the right direction. He shouldn't be asked to go far before he's on the dummy. Gradually lengthen both the distance he must travel and the distance you are from the dog when you signal.

Finally, start by giving him a line, stopping him when he's out where the dummy is hidden, some distance off to the left or right. When he swivels and plunks down at your whistle signal and looks to you for orders, send him in the proper direction. Give him the wind's benefit at first, so that if he starts properly he'll have a chance of smelling it and will home into it. Later, when he trusts you to put him on the bird, make him go downwind.

If you want the kind of precise response that will allow you to put the dog right on a bird via signals, you must demand instant response, and never let him hunt around aimlessly once he gets some distance away from you, just because he might stumble across his bird. But this is precision work. It should be done only with a dog that has some actual hunting behind him and loves it, lest he become too dependent upon the handler and too mechanical in performance, and fail to show the initiative of a good hunting dog.

For a more casual, and less intensive and time-consuming means of teaching a dog his directional signals, one which will be rather slipshod in comparison to the performance that can be elicited with the above training method but still satisfactory to most hunters, please turn to the spaniel training section.

# 10

## Training the Spaniel

To paraphrase the claim that women like to make, the spaniel's work is never done.

These bustling finders, flushers and fetchers of game are expected to "do it all" in the field. If a pointing dog retrieves, this calls for a special commendation, for he is a bird-finding specialist. And when a retriever works before the gun to produce birds, he rates special mention too, since his forte is fetching what's shot. But the spaniel—Springer, Cocker or American Water—does the whole bit and no one blinks an eye. It's expected of him.

Because so much is expected of a spaniel, turning out a really high-gloss performer requires a lot of time and persistent effort. But the happy thing about the situation is this:

Thanks to the spaniel's natural proclivities, the trainer can do a half-butted job and still be able to kill some birds over the dog, which is the important thing to the bulk of the hunters who use dogs. So just how far you apply the training tips offered here will be your choice.

Basically, a hunting spaniel need be taught just two things. The most important is to restrict his search for birds to nominal shotgun range.

Since the spaniel dashes in to put birds into the air, it's obviously going to be a wasted day—no matter how many birds are seen—if they are all flushed too far out to allow the gunner a fair crack at them.

The second requirement for a spaniel is retrieving. To find out how to go about this, I'll ask that you turn to the retriever section, just as I have asked retriever trainers to read the spaniel section on the best way to teach their breeds to hunt within gun range. The basic obedience commands the retrievers must learn should also be taught to spaniels, and in much the same manner, along with the introductions to water, gunfire and so forth.

Modifications of this pattern are included in the spaniel training section, but for the most part the training is very similar. The man who can train a retriever will do all right with a spaniel, and vice versa.

## WHEN TO START

From the time your spaniel is three to four months old you should be letting him tag along in the woods, fields and game cover. If you've followed the procedures outlined in the retriever section, your spaniel has been started on his retrieving, knows his name, comes when called

A mallard makes a mighty big mouthful for a little English Springer, but the author's *Flirt* is bringing this one in at a trot!

and pretty well responds to "No!", "Kennel!" and "Sit!" (Most spaniel trainers prefer "Hup!" to "Sit!" but it's not the word that's important, it's the response.) The "Heel!" and "Hunt 'em Out!" come a bit later, when the pup is more mature and has had a chance to develop some independence.

Confidence and independence are part and parcel of what you are trying to develop in your jaunts afield with your still immature puppy. Because spaniels are both precocious and willing to learn there is often a tendency to start demanding serious obedience too soon, to the detriment of the dog's spirit and dash when he's older.

Spaniels must hunt to the gun and obey commands with alacrity. But they cannot be totally dependent upon the handler and overly subservient, and still be capable and pleasing gun dogs. To avoid this danger, independence must be encouraged in early life, and lapses in obedience should be treated tolerantly when they're recognized as sheer puppy foolishness or animal exuberance and desire, rather than out-and-out defiance of authority. But one must be careful with adult dogs. They need a firm hand lest they gain the upper hand in an exceedingly pleasant but wily way. Spaniels have the facility of making a man feel like Simon Legree when he disciplines them. So have your fun with the puppy and require obedience from the mature dog.

While in the field, let your spaniel puppy *be* a puppy until he is six to eight months of age. If his instincts are correct, he'll teach himself many things in this manner, among them how to use his nose. Take him into game cover and let him find, flush and chase whatever is available. This includes field sparrows, meadow larks, rabbits or anything else that leaves scent and flies or runs. At this age there's little likelihood he'll "take off" on you. You're his buddy, and he's going to keep an eye on you for he's not quite so sure of himself as he may appear.

## WALKING WITH A PURPOSE

When you take your pup out, *do not walk aimlessly, or in a straight line.* Set a zig-zag course in your hikes, walking to and into likely-looking cover clumps, guiding your pup into low marshy spots, along fence-rows, and into other places where game is likely to be found. Walk as you would when hunting. This will help to establish the hunting pattern the dog will follow in later life, namely, quartering uniform cover and breaking the quartering pattern to investigate likely spots. As he gains confidence, and his legs get stronger and begin to carry him out of gun range, change your direction each time he reaches the limits, speak his name, and blow two beeps on the whistle while walking away from him. Unless he's hot on scent, he'll turn and come along with you. In time this nubbin of the idea of working in front of you will be ready for development as habit.

At six to eight months your spaniel should be a happy and sure mover in the field, and ready for some serious training to supplement what he has learned casually up to now. His introduction to guns, feathers, retrieving etc. has all been explained in the retriever training section. This should be behind him. Now you can teach him to "Heel!"—which will play a big part in his learning manners before the gun—and to "Hunt 'em Out!" which will be used to encourage his bird-finding instincts. Both procedures are outlined in the retriever section.

You'll have to stay up close, when your spaniel is working birds, if you want to get a shot.

## HUNTING IN GUN RANGE

Continue to take your pup afield, and do some of your basic training there as well as in the yard at home. But by now, he's going to be less concerned with keeping in touch with you than in having a ball. He'll be kiting out of gun range from time to time. Allow him to run all he wants to in the field, as long as he stays within gun range (thirty-five to forty yards) crisscrossing in front of you. In uniform cover, the ideal pattern might be described as an arc, twenty-five yards or less to the front and no more than forty yards to each side.

As soon as he lines out straight and gets beyond gun range, call him in to you and put him at heel. Keep him at heel for a minute or so, then release him and encourage him to "Hunt 'em Out!" As long as he stays within range, let him work, using only words of encouragement and occasional "beep beeps" on the whistle when you make abrupt changes in direction, so that you turn him and keep him moving across your front. As you alert your dog and make your turns, wave your arm in the new direction. This will start him responding to hand signals. The minute he takes the bit in his teeth, call him back in to heel. Keep repeating this procedure.

Without a whole lot of running after your dog, or cussing and whistle blowing, in a short time your pup will have picked up the idea that if he moves in a certain pattern at a certain distance from you, he can have fun. When he doesn't he has to heel—and no really spirited dog actually likes to heel.

Many spaniels possess a strong instinct to quarter before the gun, and will pick up this habit with virtually no effort on your part. With the retrievers more time and effort is usually necessary, since fewer of them possess this instinct; they're inclined to either line out too far, or be content to walk at heel.

If you have a retriever that you're training to hunt as a spaniel does (thereby greatly increasing his usefulness and your pleasure in him) by all means use this method of developing his independent intelligence while preserving reasonable control. Let your retriever put in a season or two on game, before starting with the strict control that's needed to instill the mechanical response to handling outlined in the retriever section.

During this early training of your spaniel or retriever, work into the wind wherever possible. It will greatly simplify matters, since a dog's natural tendency is to use the wind, but since few dogs care to head straight into a breeze, it encourages quartering.

## FINDING BIRDS

Let's hope you've had your spaniel or retriever afield enough so that he's bumped into some real birds. Because now, we're going to give him some work on some *un*real ones, the same wing-covered or scent-impregnated retrieving dummies he marked and fetched when they were thrown for him.

Now, however, we're going to hide the dummies in cover, and then walk through it in our hunting manner and let the dog "home in" on the scent, "catch the bird," and bring it to us. This is not a very complicated procedure. Just scatter several retrieving dummies about the field, and work your dog toward them into the wind.

He should bounce in on the dummies and bring them to you happily. When he does, praise him highly. If he's in the vicinity of the dummy but doesn't seem to be working the scent, keep him there, tell him to "Hunt 'em Out!" and stick with it until he finds it.

By using the dummies in this manner you can instill the desired response to your "Hunt 'em Out!" command because you know the dog's reward for redoubled effort—the dummy—is there. Then when you are hunting, and you suspect that he may have passed up a bird or is having trouble on a retrieve, you can ask him to "Hunt 'em Out!" Even if he fails to produce, the habit will be so strongly instilled that he won't resent your "fooling" him.

## RING IN REAL BIRDS

Once he finds these dummies independently, with your encouragement, you can start to ring birds into these training sessions. Dizzy and plant some pigeons, as outlined in the retriever section; or if you can afford to, use game birds. Use the dummies from now on for "brush-up work," but don't overdo it. Alternate with real birds to keep him really interested.

Kill the birds he flushes, either doing your own shooting or having a companion do it, but making sure that the eager pup doesn't get sprinkled as he chases a low-flying bird. For chase he will, and should. When he picks up the downed bird, have him fetch and deliver properly —as you have taught him in the yard-training sessions outlined in the retriever section. Praise him highly. Have some "game" out there (even if it's only dummies) so that his searching efforts are rewarded at least a couple times while you are working him.

However, don't plant so many birds that your dog will have trouble moving about without falling over one. He should learn early that it takes work to produce a bird. Also, since your pup is not yet steady to wing and shot, when you are using pigeons or other actual birds he could get messed up with the other planted birds when chasing a flyer. So put 'em down one at a time.

## TAKE HIM HUNTING

As of right now, your spaniel is ready to go hunting. If the season is on you, by all means take him. He can't get too much of this (he'll seldom get enough) and if he does get away with some shenanigans or develops a bad habit or two, they can always be dealt with. So don't lose a day in the field with him just because he isn't fully trained. It's hunting, and only hunting, that will make him birdwise—something which all the yard and field training you can do won't accomplish.

The little Springer bitch who graces my kennel right now flushed and fetched her first woodcock at the tender age of five months. What formal training she received came after the hunting season closed, and in effect she broke herself, and learned about birds and hunting during the actual season. When I'm taking a shooting party out or am hard pressed to find birds, she's the dog I put down; for despite lapses in manners, as a bird-finding little dynamo she's hard to equal. Don't count on getting a pup like this, but if you do get one recognize it, and use the pup and enjoy him.

Once this dashing little devil of yours starts to provide you with some shooting, he'll also present you with problems. If you're like me you won't do much about it during the hunting season, because you'll be too interested in hunting. Besides, this should be a post-season operation, after the pup has a season of hunting firmly imbedded in his memory.

## PROBLEMS

I'm pretty sure I can guess what your two major complaints are going to be, not because I'm so damn smart, but because I found out by doing.

One gripe runs something like this: "Sure, he stays in gun range—until he hits a running bird (usually pheasant). Then he goes like hell and puts the bird up on the other side of the field, and I don't get a shot."

The second one sounds like: "When he *did* get a bird up close enough for me to shoot and I missed, he shagged the son of a gun right out of the country, and then chased up another one (or maybe two or three) out of range while I was waiting for him to come back."

There are, obviously, three possible solutions to these problems. Either run faster, shoot better or teach your dog to stop on command. While I can't help you with your sprinting or shooting, let's try with the dog.

## CONTROL IN THE FIELD

If you've ever watched a field trial for spaniels, you know that the control handlers can exercise over these dogs is phenomenal. So it can be done. However, field trials require perfection, something a hunting dog seldom achieves. You can, however, bring your dog under reasonable control so he won't foul up your shooting.

Your dog should know that a sharp whistle blast or a shouted command ("Whoa," "Hup," "Wait"—take your choice) means "stop and sit, *right now*." I say he should know this and obey if you've followed the procedure outlined in the retriever section. Now it's a matter of making it stick under hunting conditions.

I'll have to assume that around the yard and under normal conditions, your spaniel (or retriever) will plunk his fanny down no matter where he is in relation to you on one blast of the whistle, an upraised arm, or a verbal command. But under the stress of birds getting up and guns going off, he ignores or just "doesn't hear" while hunting.

Put him down in the training field in light cover. Take your dummies and a blank pistol with you. While he is working busily, shoot a blank in the air. He'll look. Hit him with that sharp whistle blast and throw your arm upright. He should sit down. If he doesn't, get out there on the double and *make* him sit. Keep him there for a few moments. Then, release him with an "All Right, Hunt 'em Out!" and wave your arm, right or left, as you move out in that direction. If he goes opposite to the way you indicated, stop him with the whistle. Repeat the command and signal, and do so until he starts off in the direction you indicated.

(Yes, we're doubling-up here. Your dog is also getting worked on taking directional signals. With continued work on this you'll be able to send your dog over into a piece of cover you want worked out, but which he may have bypassed, with a wave, backed up by a "Hunt 'em Out!" encouragement. A lot of your hunting buddies will be not only impressed but pleased when your dog responds to this, and produces a bird from a place that might otherwise have remained undisturbed.)

When the gunshot makes your dog anticipate the whistle blast so that he stops and starts to sit, bring out the dummies. Shoot, throw, whistle and gesture. Even though he's been sitting for gunfire, he may break when he sees the dummy in the air. So throw it where you can intercept him on his way to it, if he breaks for it. Grab him, take him back to where he should have sat, plunk him down, and scold and shake him.

A very effective way to punish a dog is to grasp the loose skin on both sides of the neck and give a couple of hard shakes—doesn't a bitch discipline her pup similarly?

Then go back to your original post and signal the dog to fetch. If he's forgotten about the dummy, direct him to the area with whistle and hand signals. You've lost nothing and the practice is good for him. Praise when he completes.

However, if he plunked down and didn't break, keep him steady for a few moments, and then send him to fetch and complete in the normal manner. You'll probably be able to do this in one series of lessons, spread over an hour or two's walk with your dog. Every now and then from here on, hold him in a steady position for quite some time, so that there's no doubt in his mind that he should stay pinned until sent.

On the same hike, make him do some stopping without gunfire or dummies. When he's working busily, hit him with the whistle. Then when he stops and sits (make him if he doesn't) hold him as you walk toward him, and cast him off with a release command and a wave of your arm straight out. Insist that he move off in the direction you indicate. This is the start of being able to stop him on the line of a hot-footing pheasant and let you close the gap between the dog and yourself at a walking pace and have a chance for a shot.

Mix this all up for variety in training and to teach the dog to recognize that he is to start his retrieve only from a sitting position and on signal, and that a shot and a bird in the air means "assume the position." When he has it down pat on dummies—whether it takes two sessions or twenty —move up to live birds.

## STEADYING ON LIVE BIRDS

For this work you should enlist a helper who is a good shot. Use either pigeons or game-farm birds, the former being cheaper and more readily available. Plant them as you did during your pup's basic training. Let him flush a few, and allow them to fly without being shot at. When he puts his bird up, hit him with the whistle blast. If he plunks down, wonderful! Go tell him how great he is, then send him on.

If not, *get on him*. He knows what that whistle blast means—he's defying you. Let him know how unhappy you are, loud and clear. If you can't catch him, wait until he comes back, take him to the place he flushed and make him sit there for a while. Then move on to the next bird. When he'll stay steady for the flying bird with no shot, bring the gun into play. Don't try to shoot the bird yourself, for you'll have your head and hands full with the dog. Have your partner do the gunning.

Sometimes the birds that you allowed to fly free (especially pigeons) will come winging back over you. No sense wasting them. Sit your dog and have your partner drop the bird. Watching a bird in flight, or only hearing the shot and marking the fall at different angles is good practice for the dog. But of course, keep him steady. That's what he's there for.

There's a good reason for starting your steadying on game without any shooting. If you shoot the bird and your dog breaks, the odds are that he'll be on the bird before you can get to him or it. Then you *can't* punish him and put him in his place, but must let him retrieve and praise him for it, just as you did when you were hunting him and he acquired this habit. Get it? You don't want to cut down his desire, or confuse him about his fetching duties.

## WHEN SINNING IS SATISFACTORY

You may be among the large number of hunters who would be willing to stop right here. In other words, when a bird flies and there's no shooting (as with a hen pheasant, for example) you'd want the dog to stay put. Perhaps, however, you'd rather have the dog break shot and would accept a chase when a bird is missed, figuring that by breaking shot your dog will also get on a crippled bird faster. There is merit in this. If you want to accept this degree of work, it's okay with me, and I sure won't fault a hunting dog for doing this.

In fact, as you'll read later in the pointing-dog section, if the gun dog is a pointer or setter, I'm all for shot-breaking as a practical matter, particularly on pheasants; not being particularly good markers or trailers, pointing dogs need all the advantage they can get. However, a retriever or spaniel doesn't need this edge—he'll work out a cripple's trail if he's any good. Furthermore, if a couple of birds get out and both are shot— not frequent, but at the same time not unusual—the steady spaniel or retriever will be able to mark the falls of both.

## STEADY UNDER GUNFIRE

The routine when steadying under the gun is much the same as steadying to wing, and in fact is just an extension of it. If your dog breaks to make a retrieve, use every means possible to halt him—whistling, hollering or intercepting—*before he gets to the bird.* If you don't get him stopped, write it off as a loss and start over, accepting his delivery without comment. You can't punish him or scold him, but there's no sense letting him think you're really happy with this defiance. If you *do* stop him before he reaches the bird, drag him back, and make him sit steady until you send him, handling him if he has a memory lapse.

If all goes well at first and he *does not* break shot, don't hold him too long at first, but send him as soon as the bird hits the ground. You can work on longer holds later.

Your gunner is very important. Make sure he's the collected type who

To steady a Springer Spaniel, place yourself between the spot where the dummy will land and the sitting dog, so that you can intercept the dog if he breaks to make the retrieve.

will pass up a shot if there's the remotest danger to you or the dog. If he knows something about dogs and their training, so much the better— as long as he keeps his mouth shut while you're training. But at least he should understand that if the dog goes with the bird he should hold his fire. It'll make the training job easier if he shoots only when the dog is sitting steady.

## WHY THIS WAY?

There are those who will disagree with this procedure and claim a dog should be completely yard-broke and steady before he is hunted. I couldn't disagree more. You want a hunting dog. If he has a portion of the "hunt" knocked out of him through discouragement and discipline before he ever discovers what the game is really about, you'll never put it back. You can knock the knot-headed performance and mistakes out of most dogs, but you can't instill or restore desire in a single one. Besides, you're a hunter first and a dog trainer second. You bought the dog to hunt with him. If you're going to wait until you get him trained to perfection, you'll be missing out on a lot of hunting and it's likely your dog will never get into the field.

So don't worry about having a completely "broke dog" until after he's had a season or two of hard hunting, with plenty of birds. Even then you may find that you are satisfied with him as he is, and that's what counts. If you do decide to exercise rigid control early, you can crack down fairly quickly on a tough, aggressive dog, but you should go easy on the soft, overly conscientious one.

## RUNNING BIRDS

You can finish off your dog's performance in handling running birds by releasing a wing-clipped pheasant or a domestic mallard and having him trail it, insisting that he stop and wait for you on command, picking up the trail again after you've closed up the distance, and finally letting him catch it when you are in gun range.

But use some judgement in all of this. If your whistling and halting him seems to interfere with his interest in hunting, lay off for a while. You want a responsive dog, but not one that's looking over his shoulder in anticipation of being handled.

## WATER WORK

By all means give your spaniel plenty of work in water, following the same introduction and training procedure outlined in the retriever section. Unless weather or water conditions are extreme, your spaniel should be able to handle all the ducks the present law allows you to shoot. This applies to the American Water (which was developed for the hunter working out of a duck skiff) the Springer, and even the Cocker to some extent. Besides, upland game is often found in wet marshes or near water when weather or shooting pressure so dictates and a water-busting spaniel is a prime partner for this kind of work.

## PRECISE HANDLING

Spaniels can be taught precise handling commands just as the retrievers can (see retriever section), but for the most part, the hunter will be satisfied if his spaniel or retriever responds by going in the general direction of an arm wave, as he has been trained to do as outlined in this section. Do work, however, at making sure he'll cross a creek, ditch or obstacle when waved on, rather than turning, as is natural when the going gets tough.

## FACE FACTS

Finally, let's face a couple of facts about going hunting with spaniels and retrievers. One, there are going to be times when you simply must stir your stumps to get to within gun range of your flush-dog before he puts his bird into the air. This is particularly true with pheasants, which often flush some distance out in front of the dog.

You won't always be able to mosey along because no dog really produces pheasants unless he pushes them *hard*. A slow-working, cautious dog may lead you through a half-mile of cover and never produce a bird, or else have it lift some distance out in front of him when it tires of running. So resign yourself to some occasional hot-footing and stay on your toes when your spaniel or retriever is making game; but accept some wild flushes, particularly in light cover.

Don't ever call your spaniel off a hot line, as is sometimes done in field trials. You may confuse your dog or cause a crippled bird to get away. Stop him, if you can, and send him on. In field trials there are other birds planted to test the dog and he must stay on a prescribed beat. In the hunting field, however, the one bird your spaniel is pushing so hard (even if he doubles around behind you) may be the only one you'll see all day. You can't afford to pass it up, and form and manners may have to suffer to produce it.

Accept, also, the fact that few real hard-going, all-day hunting dogs who don't know the word "quit" are ever going to be completely steady. Some, with much experience or some special insight, will be selective about when they break. An English Cocker of mine would watch hens fly off, but would chase pheasant roosters out of sight. As a matter of conscience and candid confession, perhaps I'm asserting this because I've never had a spaniel or retriever I completely trusted to stay steady.

True, spaniels in field trials are rock-steady. If you ever get the opportunity, go see a field trial, so you'll have an idea what really superlative dog work is. But by way of explanation, or to excuse our own dog's performance, there is a reason for this control even beyond excellent and intensive training.

The handler in the field trial is just that. His only responsibility is the dog and he concentrates on a dog. Official guns knock the birds down. A dog seems to sense when you're "on him," and even if he decides to defy his handler the alert handler can anticipate it, or catch him quick enough with a command to hold him.

Not so the hunter. He has to shoot a bird. That takes concentration. The dog senses that he isn't being watched. Take your eyes off him for a couple of seconds as you swing on the birds and he's gone. Who's going to discipline him as he comes trotting back to you, bird in mouth? Not me. Not you. He knows he can get away with it, and he does.

So in conclusion, nobody is going to cuss your dog—much—if he breaks shot, as long as you are able to stop him within a reasonable distance should you miss. I'd say a reasonable distance is up to forty yards, gun range. That's about as well-broke a dog as most of us will develop.

But if you want a real treat, wangle yourself an invite to hunt behind a couple of retired Springer Spaniel field-trial champs who have had a season or two of actual hunting following retirement from competition. Then let that kind of performance be your goal, unattainable for most, in spaniel hunting excellence.

# 11

## Training the Pointing Breeds

Pointing dogs are best trained by giving them the widest possible latitude to "do what comes naturally." But in common with all flat statements about dogs, this has to be qualified.

To begin with, this remark might lead you to believe that pointing dogs are easier to train than spaniels or retrievers. They aren't. Even when the dog is well trained, the handler must resign himself to occasional lapses and "those days" when a pointer or setter is just "off." Seldom does one achieve the consistency of performance and bird production with a pointing dog that is possible with a spaniel or retriever, for a number of reasons that will become self-evident as we go along.

In fact, is is harder for an amateur to train a pointing dog, for one simple reason: very few have the time and facilities to allow their pointing protégés to "do what comes naturally." To develop properly, a pointing-dog prospect must put in a lot of time in game cover containing birds. If those requirements should be available to you, you'll get supreme thrills and untold enjoyment out of working with a pointer or setter, and can develop him into a first-class hunting companion.

112

If not—if shooting birds is more important to you than watching a dog work—stick with the spaniels or retrievers. They can be basically trained by artificial methods plus whatever exposure to actual game and hunting cover you can furnish.

You take a flushing dog hunting; a pointing dog *takes you*. He must eventually be controlled and trained, true. But because of his natural instincts and the fact that he is (or should be) a much greater distance from his handler when hunting than the flusher, his response to commands will not be as instantaneous and mechanical.

It's axiomatic that the promptness of a dog's responses are directly related to his proximity to the handler. A dog quickly recognizes that if you say "Whoa!" when standing alongside him, you'll be able to enforce that command by restraint, a swat or a shaking-up. He also learns that when he's some distance from you, you are in a poor position to enforce commands, and he then responds only through desire to please, as a confirmation of habits instilled by diligent repetition.

## HAPPY-MEDIUM DOG

One blustery winter afternoon, a friend who has had some success with field-trial pointers and setters in the thirty-minute, planted-bird field trials common to the northern states, pulled into the yard.

Not one step further! This pointer is showing us that the birds are right *there*.

"Hear you got a couple of new Pointer pups, real good breeding," was all he had to say. I took him out to the kennel for a look.

When I opened the kennel gate, two nine-month-old Pointers dashed out and my friend made a frantic but futile attempt to grab both at the same time. He shouted, "Quick! Catch 'em! They'll get away!" Knowing the cause for his concern, I couldn't help being deliberately casual as I asked, "Why? They aren't going any place." But by this time they were kiting into the woods, half-a-quarter away. Fortunately they swung back to us, and gamboled about as I talked to them and teased while we were walking out to the frozen lake in front of the house.

When we reached the lake, I said, "All right. Get Back!" and waved them out. They started reaching and soon were only specks on the frozen surface. I started blowing the whistle. They swung and as I continued blowing, they finally came loping into me. I petted and talked to them and walked them back to the kennel. "I'll be darned," my friend said. "They run like hell, but they don't run away."

Field-trial dogs are expected to "run big." To encourage this my friend was in the habit of virtually letting his dogs run wild, and they were never let out except when he was actually working them in the field. They were often lost, and he either waited until they were tired enough to come in, or went out and tried to catch them; sometimes he was missing a dog for a day or more. When his pups were this age, it was his firm conviction that they should do little else but run, the farther the better. He refused to do anything that might "interfere with their running." This obviously is not practical for the man who wants to hunt with a dog, and as soon as possible.

On the other hand, I've had to bite my tongue when hunting with another man and his dog, to keep from saying something when his dog never worked beyond the range of a open-bored shotgun and was almost underfoot half the time, having to be constantly urged to get out and snuffle around in the cover. This is too prevalent among the Continental pointing breeds. I don't want to spend ten minutes in the field with a dog like that, much less a season, or a half-dozen valuable seasons in my lifetime.

Just as there are hot-blooded, high-strung dogs who are virtually impossible to hold down, so are there phlegmatic individuals who just won't or can't stir their stumps. However, in many instances, the training is at fault. Dogs can be made into terrific, wildly abandoned runners (not hunters) by working them in open, barren country where they have to run if they're to find any game at all, and by forcing them out with whip or shouting, or pushing their running pace with a fast horse.

They can also be made into overly-dependent "shoe-polishers" by some of the newly-advocated training methods which exercise rigid control over the pointing dog long before he has had any field experience, placing all the emphasis on intensive formal and artificial training, often called "yard-breaking."

What I hope you and I can do is to develop a dog that strikes a happy medium between these extremes—a bold, independent hunter with an attractive way of going, who is still reasonably biddable to the guidance of his handler and thus maintains contact with the gun; a dog you can shoot birds over, yet whose desire and intensity will still thrill you.

Admittedly, whether or not we succeed will depend not only on our abilities as trainers and our diligent application of the training methods, but to a great degree on the dog's natural abilities.

## BASIC COMMANDS

The pointer and setter can be taught all the commands that a retriever or spaniel must learn—(see retriever section for what and how) —or you can skip some of them. But whatever you decide, the pointing dog need know only two commands before he is taken out for field experience, aside from responding to his name; they are:

1) To come when called by voice or whistle.

2) The equivalent of "Wait!", "Stay!" or "Hup!", which in pointing-dog parlance is "Whoa! The pointing dog "Whoas" in a standing position rather than at a sit, and it may be preferable to forget entirely the "Sit!" command on the off-chance that may affect a dog's style when on point.

With few exceptions, mastery of the other commands should be delayed until the pup has enjoyed a lot of freedom in the field and has established stanch points. This is particularly true of retrieving, although some play-training will do no great harm, and may make easier or virtually eliminate the necessity for force-training later on.

The "Whoa!" can be taught in much the same manner as the retriever's "Wait!" (See retriever section). However, you may prefer an equally effective and perhaps more practical method. When you set your dog's food in front of him, tell him "Whoa!" and restrain him with your hands. When you say "All Right!" pat him on the head and let him eat. This can also be done with morsels of food laid down in front of him. Then when you have him out for some exercise and play, and he's scampering around close enough for you to catch, "Whoa!" him.

If he stops, praise him, walk up and stroke him and then tap his head and say, "All Right!" releasing him to move out. This conditioning will prove valuable when you start teaching him his manners on game. He'll know the command he is expected to obey, he'll be used to having your hands on him and will have learned that a pat on the head and the release command mean it's all right to move out to relocate, or to start hunting afresh. Obedience to this "Whoa!" will also enable you to stop him from shagging after missed shots or wild-flushing birds, and will help to teach him to back (honor the point of another dog).

If he doesn't stop on the command, catch him and stand him in the spot in which you wanted him to stop. If he persists in defying you, you may introduce him to the check-cord, a long length of rope attached to his collar. Let him run to the end of this rope and say "Whoa!" and if he does not stop, jerk the rope sharply, repeating "Whoa!" It won't take too many jerks on the neck (or an occasional tipping over when he hits the end of the rope hard) to get him to come to a halt when commanded. You may not have to do this. But if he is a "hardhead" and ignores you, work on him. Then let him run without the rope and "Whoa!" him. If he doesn't respond, go back to the check-cord until he does. Wearing gloves will save sore hands.

## PRELIMINARY FIELD WORK

From the age of about six months on, get your pup into the field as frequently as possible—every day for an hour or so, if you can swing it.

Dave Duffey nails a chukar partridge over his German Wirehair's point.

Don't just walk about aimlessly. Act as though you were hunting and put him down in the kind of country he'll be working in. Try to work him out in different places as much as possible so that he'll become accustomed to new vistas and will develop a knowledge of how to hunt objectively, going to spots that are likely to hold birds.

When you're walking (or riding a horse) with your dog moving well out in front of you, try to anticipate when he is going to change direction or break his cast. Then "beep, beep" him on the whistle (two beeps for the turn signal; a series of trills or harsh blasts as occasion demands, means "come in") and swing in the direction you want to go, waving your arm. Chances are good he'll swing that way in an effort to keep in front of you and make a big loop. Don't get disgusted and quit if he doesn't do it right away; keep at it. Don't wave him aimlessly back and forth across a pasture or other barren piece of ground. Have some objective that he'll be inclined to head for each time you ask him to swing, such as a brush pile, cover clump, stand of trees or similar place where game might be.

I can't overemphasize the importance of making a buddy of your dog at home and in the kennel as a means of making this training easier. If you succeed, he'll follow his instincts to range and hunt but he'll still want to keep track of you. This will materially aid his handling response. He may even come back to check with you quite frequently. Occasional returning to the hunter is not at all objectionable in a hunting dog, and it may even be desirable, provided that the dog does not go out and return on virtually the same track. Once he's covered a piece of ground and searched out the cover, there's no point in going over it again. When he loops into you, don't make a big fuss over him (lest he get the idea he ought to be doing this all the time) but switch direction, wave and tell him to "Hunt 'em Out!" or "Get Back!" in the new direction.

When he's in close like that and goes off in a different direction than you've indicated, hit him with the whistle, and keep at him until he goes where you want him to. He won't learn this in a day; it may take a week, probably longer. Keep at it.

## RUN BIG OR HUNT CLOSE

If a "big-running" dog is your desire, let the pup have his head as much as possible and don't break his casts with a whistle. You may also find that running a pair of puppies together will encourage reaching out. Seldom does a close-working pup shorten the range of a wide-ranging one. The "big-goer" sucks the shorter one out. But don't overdo running a pair of pups together, particularly if one does nothing but trail the other, or if the pups indicate after a few sessions that they are more interested in just racing each other than in hunting.

If you want your dog to be a close worker (what's close is a matter of opinion, but let's say it's up to 150 yards) work him all you can in continuous, heavy cover which will either impede his going, or require that he shorten up to keep track of you. Meanwhile, use your whistle or a verbal command like "Yeeeohhh, Rip!" to keep him alert and more or less quartering in front of you. You'll find that there are "naturals" who shut down when they get into heavy cover and reach out when the objectives are scattered. If you take advantage of this, you can have a truly versatile pointing dog.

You may also help to shorten your dog's range by putting him down in very "birdy" cover where there is a lot of scent. He'll have to investigate, and as his pointing instinct comes to the fore he'll flash-point, probably doing this many times to correct erroneous impressions before he moves on or even flush and chase. This will cut down on his running.

You may also do this by artificial means, although this will probably come later when you are teaching manners. Put wing-clipped pigeons in the field in such a manner that it's possible for you to always be near them as the dog moves in and locks up. (You anticipate when the dog will work into them, and move to be near when he points.) In time, he will come to associate you with birds because of this training, and he'll hunt relatively close because he'll figure that the birds must be somewhere around you.

## COVEY OR SINGLES DOG

Because there are different natural styles of working, it is common in the quail country of the South for one to refer to a "singles dog" or a "covey dog." The covey dog reaches and is often out of sight, for he gobbles up big chunks of territory to locate widely-scattered coveys of birds. The singles dog works much closer, almost quartering his ground, and he more or less "mops up" game, finding close-sitting sleepers or scattered singles that may be separated from the main body of birds. With his greater range and speed, the covey dog might pass these birds or a tight-sitting covey.

Run together, such dogs can complement each other. But if a choice must be made, the hunter who works the big plantation and prairie type of cover will probably favor a "covey dog." The man tramping thick restricted coverts, where a dog is difficult to keep track of and locate when on point (as in the East and Midwest) will prefer a dog patterned after the singles dog. A dog that likes to run is hard to keep

Retrieving dogs and pointing dogs can be worked together. Harry Stroebe's setter (shown above with his owner) did the pointing on this ruffed grouse hunt, while Dave Duffey's two Labradors did the retrieving.

in, and one whose natural range is closer is hard to push out. If you are lucky enough to get the kind you want, your training job is going to be greatly simplified.

You should know, however, that while diligent effort and hacking can cut down the range of a dog before he drives you out of your mind, very little can be done to make a dog hunt the horizon if his natural inclination is to be more deliberate and investigative.

## THE NAME OF THE GAME

Bird hunting is the name of the game. If a pointing dog doesn't find birds, there's no point in feeding him. That's why I recommend giving the dog field work and some contact with birds before spending a lot of time teaching him commands and a lot of money maintaining him. It also develops his independence.

No matter how well he obeys or what an appealing personality he has, if he lacks the physical stamina to run hard, or the discerning nose to locate game and the desire to produce for you, you're money ahead to get rid of him and start over. Fortunately, most bird dogs from field stock can be counted on to have the proper instincts and physical requirements.

Your chances of getting a "lemon" are high, however, if you get a pointer or setter from show stock, or prefer one of the breeds that hasn't distinguished itself in the field for many generations. By following the procedure I've outlined, you'll find out early if you are lucky enough to have one that has retained the hunting acumen of his ancestors. If you are unfortunate, don't be squeamish about it. The idea is to save you money and time.

Every dog will have some faults, and some develop much slower than others. Every dog deserves a chance. But if this pup of yours is, in effect, just one big "Blah!" put both the dog and yourself out of your miseries by keeping him only as a pet, or giving him to someone. In hopeless cases, the most humane thing to do is to put the dog down.

A dog of virtually any breed can be taught to point, if you are willing to accept a "stand" on game. But a pup that doesn't show pointing instinct when he encounters wild bird-scent isn't any more promising a prospect than the retriever or spaniel who won't pick up and carry until he's extensively force-trained.

## FUN AND GAMES

There is one stunt, however, that will do no harm and perhaps some good, as it will give you a line on the pup's intelligence and temperament and let you get in some licks on your "Whoa!" training.

Get a cane pole or fly rod, and tie on a fishline of equal length. Tie a bird wing on the end of the line. Let the pup see and smell it as it lies on the ground, once you've attracted his attention to it. If he pounces at it, "fly" the bird away by lifting it into the air, and then land it in front of him again. If the pup's instinct is strong, he'll soon start pointing the wing, sight-pointing it. If he softens on point, twitch

A dead pigeon, tied to the end of a fishline and manipulated by a pole, can be used to attract and entice a pointing-dog puppy and bring him to an intense point, as with this German Wirehaired Pointer.

it along the ground in front of him. He'll get intent again. Praise and stroke him. If he moves up too fast, caution him with a soft, "Whoaaa-uupp!" and try to halt him with a sharp "Whoa!" if he breaks. Should he catch the bird now and then, no harm; this is a game for puppies and a not too interested pup may be made more eager by doing some catching. As a rule, however, get the bird into the air and out of his reach when he rushes it.

You can do this in your yard before you ever take your pup afield, and may continue it into his later months. But you'll find that the more intelligent pup will quickly tire of this game and either refuse to point intensely, or ignore it entirely, particularly after he's had a noseful of the real thing. Others will go on performing this stunt all their lives. (Very often they are confirmed sight-pointers who don't shine in the field but can be used for staged exhibitions or picture taking.) Everyone will "oh and ah" over this puppy trick and there are some training benefits to be derived from it; but continue it only as long as the pup shows interest.

## WILD GAME

Native game in natural habitat isn't easy to find. But as a hunter you may know of some good bird-country that is open, or perhaps you belong to a shooting club that features the hunting of released game birds. As a last resort, you may have to "plant your own," which is most artificial, but your only recourse if you are going to give your dog experience and make him mannerly.

By all means try to get this pup in contact with real game before you start hunting him. Unlike the spaniel and retriever, a pointing dog should know about game before you even shoot over him. How much time, work and travel will be involved in providing this depends upon your location. But no matter how good or diligent a trainer you are, without real game your dog will never reach the level he'd attain in the hands of a trainer only half as talented, but who has game cover containing birds at his disposal, and whose pointer or setter can learn by doing.

So get your dog into cover. You'll increase your chances of getting some bird work by doing your field training in the early morning and evening. This time of day, when birds are most likely to be moving about and giving off scent, also coincides with the time of day when most men are free from the chore of earning a daily living.

Do not work your dog on natural game in nesting cover during the nesting season (generally late spring and early to mid-summer). You'll disturb game that shouldn't be disturbed and destroy nests, and your pup may catch weak-flying young birds. This is bad from a conservation standpoint, and it's not good for the young dog, either.

You can continue to work your dog by planting or releasing game-farm birds, pigeons, and so on in some area you know is barren of birds.

## FIRST CONTACTS

Your pup's first contacts with birds will probably result in one of two things. He'll either snap into a flash point (a momentarily held response to an age-old instinct) and then jump in and try to catch the birds; or he'll get very interested in the scent, beat his tail merrily, and move right into and go with the birds. The first is preferable, but the second isn't bad. At this stage about the only thing he can do wrong is ignore birds—and even then, don't give up. Get him back to the spot from which the birds lifted, and encourage him to sniff around. You may even tell him to "Whoa!" downwind of where the birds were, in an effort to get him to connect paying attention and stopping with hitting scent.

Occasionally he will hold his point even after flush, if the bird or birds get up wild, allowing enough time for you to get up and get your hands on him. If you're lucky enough to be able to do this, hold him back with one hand on the brisket, and stroke down his back from shoulder to tail tip with the other hand, murmuring "Whoaaauuuppp, Gooood Dog, Goood Boy" etc. Then tap his head and send him on, if the birds have flown. Otherwise go out and flush them. He'll probably come with you. That's okay at first too. Later on, caution him to "Whoaauuupp" until you get the birds into the air. With a pup like this you may never have to resort to a check-cord or a lot of planted-bird work to teach him manners. They do come like this; but not often enough!

At times when you are deliberately working your dog on birds you should have an assistant. Then he can flush while you concentrate on restraining the dog. However, in the early stages this isn't necessary.

It is most likely that your pup will chase. Let him. Don't run after him, screaming, shouting and whistling; you're liable to give him the idea he isn't *supposed* to find these birds. The fact is that given enough opportunity, some smart dogs learn that chasing is futile. Even though they may crowd and flush birds, they don't chase. This is particularly true after birds have been shot over them. When you have a really bold dog that you can start shooting over early, he may very well "break himself." But to play it safe, we're holding back on the shooting for a while.

When your pup has come back of his own accord (you may want to hide on him here, to impress on his mind that you're still the guy who shows him all this fun and that it's pretty big country without you) put a lead or check-cord on him and lead him back to where the birds were. "Whoa" him, and when he's standing, stroke, pet and praise as you did (or would have done) with a pup that displayed precocious stanchness.

Perhaps an explanation of terms is in order here. "Stanch" and "steady" are not the same thing. A dog is "stanch" (holds his point until the birds are flushed) on birds. He is "steady" (doesn't break point and chase, when the birds get up and a shot is fired) to wing and shot.

Some pups (your dog at this stage may be seven to eighteen months of age) get the idea quickly. With others it takes constant repetition.

When you are sure the pup is crazy about birds, you can start exercising some restraint. But before going to check-cording and steadying him, you should formally introduce him to the gun and gunfire.

When you walk in on a young dog's first points, do it from the side, where the dog can see you and hear you coming up, as Dave Duffey is doing here with his young Pointer bitch, *Twist*.

To steady the young pointer on game, it helps to move up and gently try to shove the dog into the birds, as Duffey is doing here. The dog will resist and stiffen up, assuming a firmer

Stroking and handling the young dog on point will help its steadiness and increase intensity. Talk softly and encouragingly as you do this; then step in and flush the birds.

Unless you are working with planted birds, this will have to wait until the hunting season is open. There is small chance with a pointing dog that you will bring him into his first hunting season as a trained dog. You'll have to sacrifice the first half and perhaps all of his initial season to actual training. But it pays big dividends in future years.

## GUNS GET GAME

Once a pointing dog connects gunfire with the result—a bird he can get his nose next to and his mouth on—he'll love it for life. However, the introduction to gunfire should be a bit more careful and come later in life than with a spaniel or retriever, since we can't double-up on retrieving and shooting, as is possible in yard-training the spaniel or retriever. As a rule, the well-bred pointer or setter lacks the equanimity and placidity of disposition that most good retrievers display. It's easier to make one gunshy.

There can be a casual introduction to gunfire. At feeding time, just as you put the dog's food down have someone some distance away shoot off a .22 blank. Keep this up until the pup pays no attention to it, eventually working nearer until the gun can be fired five or ten yards away without eliciting apprehension on the dog's part.

When on your jaunts afield, with the dog out and running (particularly if he's shagging a meadowlark or some other "stink bird") shoot your blank.

If he stops and looks, just keep on walking, pretending that nothing out of the ordinary happened; he'll go back to what he was doing. Ten or fifteen minutes later try a shot again. Do this a couple times each trip so he learns that the noise isn't harmful. After you're sure the .22 doesn't bother him, move up to a .410 bore or 20-gauge shotgun, and follow the same procedure.

If he should tuck his tail and come running to you, or run away, pay him "no never mind"—just keep walking as if nothing happened. But don't shoot again that day. Continue to shoot blanks around the kennel at feeding time. Try again the next time out, and keep at it until this no longer bothers him.

But not until he's had a dozen or more game-contacts when he's smelled, seen and chased birds should you formally introduce him to the gun.

Of course, I know that all this preliminary routine is on the cautious side. I've had pups that I never bothered to do this with, because I felt I knew the dog, and was sure that shooting birds over him wouldn't faze him. But until you can safely bet on this, it's far better to be conservative. Avoiding gunshyness is easy; curing it is not. Not one man in a thousand will put up with the time and tedium necessary to correct it. Introduce him properly, and you won't have to worry.

## FIRST BIRD

The hunting season is now on you. Your pup has had experience and knows what birds are, all gleaned in the off-season. He points, you walk up. All right, let's be honest—you sort of rush up there. Try, however, to be as calm as possible; your excitement can be transmitted to the dog (yes it can), and may cause him to break. Whether he's stanch enough to allow you to flush or whether he goes into his birds, shoot and *kill one.*

If it's a covey, he may follow the flying birds, ignoring the fall. If it's a single bird (most likely with pheasant, grouse or woodcock) he'll probably be on top of the bird when it hits the ground.

If he picks it up, don't get excited—even if he seems to be chewing it—or you might chase him away from you, bird in mouth. Break your gun or put it on safe, squat down and call him to you, saying "Here, Rip! Fetch!" and keep repeating and telling him what a good dog he is. Try to get him to come all the way. If he brings it somewhere near you and lays it down and you can't coax him all the way, take up the bird, pet and praise him highly. Take plenty of time.

Tease him with the bird, excite him with your voice, toss it out and tell him to "Fetch!" He probably will, at least partially.

Sure, I know he hasn't been *taught* to fetch, and I told you to wait with this; but if he shows this much natural inclination, you may be able to make an acceptable retriever of him right in the field. If you can, fine! There's nothing uniform about dogs and no special routine in training. Take advantage of every short cut you can.

If he just sniffs the bird; or picks it up, mouths it and spits it out and moves on, don't worry. Pick up your bird and get back to hunting— after you've praised him. You can begin teaching retrieving at home, later.

What about that rascal that ran off and never went to the bird? When he comes back, bring him into the downed bird headed into the wind, and tell him "Dead bird! Hunt 'em Out! Hunt Close!" or whatever term you think applicable. He may lock up and point the dead bird. This, too, is fine.

Retrieving is preferred, of course, and will be taught later. But if you keep working on this and teach your dog to "point dead" you'll save yourself considerable routine. There's no danger of chewed birds from a rough-mouthed dog, and recovery of everything except a lightly-crippled bird is assured.

A few more episodes like this and you've got yourself a huntin' dog. He's going to make mistakes—lots of them, and some deliberate, such as flushing because he sees the bird move, or he just can't wait until you get up to him. You can start cracking down by restraining him with a check-cord now; or you can ride out the hunting season, putting up with some flushes and the breaking to shot and/or wing. If you hunt with a companion, let him hog the flushing and shooting while you steady your dog; right now, the training should be more important to you than the shooting. Or you can postpone steadying him, and then use game-farm birds or pigeons after the season is over and refresh his memory again before the next season opens.

Haven't I skipped a lot of stuff? Yup, but for very good reasons.

## EXCEPTIONS AND SHORT CUTS

You can skip all kinds of things while you're hunting or working a pointing dog by yourself, and still develop a very good gun dog in many instances, if you follow one principle: shoot only when the dog has been stanch on point, or stopped to a flush that was no fault of his. This means passing up some shots and it's hard to ask a shooting partner to do it. But you, at least, should be more concerned with the dog and his future than a few extra birds in the bag.

There are plenty of dogs who will "break themselves" if you will only restrict your shooting to the times when the dog does things right. He learns that if he stays stanch he'll get a bird. If he doesn't, no dice. Everytime he *does* break and chase, get him back, scold him and stand him up where he should have held. Then send him on to hunt some more.

So if you choose, you can suspend your training at this stage, or mix it up with serious hunting, just continuing to give your dog all the experience possible. Except for retrieving (or its pointing-dead alternate), which will be discussed in a separate section everything else can be regarded as niceties and manners. However these can add a great deal to your enjoyment of a fine day's shoot, and they'll mark your dog as a finished gun dog and a gentleman. Right now you have a gem, but a diamond in the rough; if you want to polish it, read on.

But again let me emphasize that no two dogs—even from the same breed or out of the same litter—are alike, or will respond to exactly the same treatment. While routines should be followed, there are times when you should make intelligent exceptions, just as you should be quick to take advantage of short cuts that present themselves.

## BREAKING RULES

Take the two Pointer pups referred to earlier in this chapter, litter-mates out of "hot" field-trial breeding, but both destined to be gun dogs for the hunter. The male was more biddable, and stanched up fast. When turned over to his new owner at 11 months of age he was finding game, pointing staunchly, roading running pheasants intelligently and pointing dead. ("Roading" means moving up slowly in an effort to pin down running game.)

The trim little bitch was more headstrong, but she ran well, adjusted her range to cover, and was a terrific bird-finder with an inclination toward natural retrieving. Some six or seven months later I was going easy, shooting only when she did things right, and still accepting some flushes on her part.

On this particular morning, my (then) 13-year-old son Mike and I were working her on pheasants, at a commercial shooting establishment where I guided and trained dogs. It was "one of those mornings." Every bird was on the move, there was a strong wind over snow-covered ground, and we should have been doing chores instead of training dogs. But she needed work. She always held fine, as long as the bird sat— but let it move, and in she'd go.

So the first hour-and-a-half consisted of a succession of points, running birds that were flushed and chased, shouting and bawling out, and angry attempts to enforce discipline.

I was about to call her in, put her in a crate in the back of the Jeep wagon and start on another dog, when she made a nice swing and we found her over a knoll, locked-up in a mowed strip just outside the cornrow. When we hustled up I could see a rooster sitting tight in the third cornrow.

"You shoot the bird," I told my son as I circled it, trapping it between the dog and me so it wouldn't run out, while constantly cautioning and praising this intense little bitch, who seemed to be trying to make contact with the bird with her eyeballs! I was almost astraddle the bird when it started to sprint between my legs; the bitch broke and dived for it.

It must have been a ludicrous sight, me grabbing for the dog as the bird got into the air behind me, and at the same time looking to Mike to see how he'd manage to take the bird without firing over me. But I wasn't laughing.

To my amazement, Mike hadn't brought his gun up. I turned loose the dog, spun around and killed the bird going away. The bitch pounced on it, shook it, brought it back part-way and laid it down. I got to her,

praised her and turned to bawl out Mike. "Why didn't you shoot?"
I asked.

He wore a look of consternation. "You always say, 'don't shoot unless
the dog does it right.' She broke."

He was right—generally. But not this time; and I calmed down and
explained the exception to the rule.

"All morning we've been putting pressure on this dog," I explained.
"Every time she found a bird, she wound up being disciplined. Much
of the faulty work wasn't really her fault. The birds just wouldn't co-
operate. This one finally did, and she held well. It should have been
put out faster 'cause she was on point for a long time, but we messed
around; *still* she held until I kicked it out. She deserved a reward! I
sure don't want her to think there's something wrong with finding birds!
She needed this one to finish the day."

So take exception, or make exceptions to any of the training procedures I outline. But do it intelligently and with reason, after you get
to know your dog and the means for eliciting the best from him.

Now to the niceties.

## OKAY TO BREAK SHOT

A "broke dog" with good manners is both a true gentleman in the
field and a credit to his trainer. Yet a legitimate argument can always
be offered-to excuse a dog's breaking his stand on game to dash out
and retrieve. For while it's inexusable in a field trial, there is some
justification for allowing a hunting dog this leeway.

Some dogs always seem to know when a bird is hit and break for
that bird, although they remain steady when birds are flushed and no
shots taken, as with hen pheasants, for example, or when birds are
shot at and missed.

Others will start with every shot, but can be stopped within gun
range of the hunter with a "Whoa!" command. Also, some dogs will
remain steady in a field trial where the handler can concentrate on
them and caution them, but will break when the same handler switches
his attention to shooting birds. So there are various degrees of steadiness.

I'll go this far. *Reasonable* steadiness to wing—avoiding a lot of unnecessary chasing when a bird flushes wild or a dog causes an inadvertent
flush—is highly desirable, and not too difficult to instill. *Complete*
steadiness to shot—not moving through the excitement of flush and
shot, until ordered out to retrieve or to continue hunting—can't be
commended highly enough, but it is hard for a hunter to enforce, and
may even be undesirable in a hunting dog.

The last statement is based on one thing alone. If the use of a dog in the field is to be justified on the basis of sound conservation practices, the dog must either retrieve downed game or "point dead."

The plain and simple fact is that with few exceptions, pointing dogs are rather indifferent retrievers. They lack marking and tracking abilities when compared with spaniels or retrievers. It would be interesting to see a study of the eyesight of the different breeds, for from my experience, pointers and setters seem to lack the depth perception which apparently makes retrievers and spaniels good markers.

A good setter or pointer who is accustomed to working body scent can't be expected to foot-track a running cripple the way a spaniel or retriever can, and many balk at "hunting close."

Finally, when it comes to administering the "coup de grâce" and actually catching the cripple, the pointing dog is handicapped by the instinct that leads him to hesitate before moving in to grab. But in the retrieving game, he who hesitates is lost. Most spaniels and retrievers suffer from no such compunction, and drive in on birds with the idea of catching.

So a pointing dog needs every advantage he can get in dealing with the fall of the bird, dead or crippled.

What is, in effect, a sloppy job of training, whether deliberate or because time wasn't taken to do it, can provide this needed edge. The shot-breaking dog is nearer the bird when it falls and on it quicker, before it can recover and run. Since few pointing dogs have much memory for multiple falls, and the dog that is steady must be helped to the area of the falls which the hunter himself marked, there is little advantage on this score from absolute steadiness.

Despite all this, I'll tell you how to keep your dog steady, not because it is good manners, but because it is the proper, right way to do it, and a necessity if you ever put your dog down in competition.

## STEADY TO WING AND SHOT

You'll need an assistant. You are going to work the dog; he will do the flushing or shooting. Plant your pigeons or game-farm birds, or locate some wild birds. If you haven't already done so, introduce your dog to the check-cord. (You've probably used this in the same manner that I'm going to describe if your pup broke his points, defied your "Whoa!" command, and flushed before you could reach him while you were trying to staunch him. It is also discussed in the "problems" section).

Fasten the check-cord to his collar and let him go. If you think he's likely to break and flush before you can get to him, hang onto the cord's end as you work him into the bird. This isn't good bird-finding practice if you want him to run naturally—it's mechanically teaching manners. Accordingly, it may be preferable to conduct this exercise on pigeons; then if your dog is soft in temperament and resents discipline, he won't associate this "punishment" with actual game.

When the dog points, caution him, work up the check-cord towards him until you can stroke and reassure. Have your assistant flush and shoot. Use blanks here if you wish; you are not going to kill birds at first, but let them fly away, for if your dog has been hunting and breaking shot, the falling bird would be an added temptation.

Maybe he'll hold steady, but it's likely that he won't. You holler "Whoa!" at him when he goes. If he stops, wonderful. Go up, praise him and stroke him, and then tap him on the head and send him on.

If he doesn't obey, brace yourself. Pull back when he hits the end of the check-cord and tip him over. A few experiences like this and your shot breaker will either hold, or at least stop on command.

When he gets to his feet, *do not bawl hell out of him.* Just matter-of-factly drag him back by the collar, and set him up in a pointing pose to the place he should have stayed, and stroke and praise him. You want him to associate the abrupt checking as little as possible with you. If you have a reliable helper, and you have a sensitive dog who is also stubborn, you may find it wiser to let the helper do the checking while you stay out in front. Keep at this until he is reliably steady and you can then move out in front without an assistant, and flush and shoot.

Steadying to wing and shot is a more or less mechanical, repetitive process and is actually a single training step. But when you require complete steadiness to shot as well as wing, you are extending the step to a stride.

You should use your head at all times. Sometimes too much of this harsh discipline can start a dog down the path to being a "blinker," a dog that deliberately avoids birds he knows are there. This will be discussed in the "problems" section.

## STOP TO FLUSH

There is a difference between a "stop to flush" and a "flush and stop," but sometimes it's difficult to tell which is which. If there's any doubt in your mind, withhold your fire.

The "stop to flush" is no fault of the dog's. A spooky bird (or a bird the dog accidentally bumps with the wind the wrong way) gets out, and the trained dog watches it fly rather than chasing after it.

In contrast, when a dog flushes and *then* stops he has committed a sin, either by crowding too close to his birds or deliberately knocking

To avoid a flush when caught in the middle of birds during bad scenting conditions, a pointing dog may crouch rather than stand high-stationed, just as this German Shorthair is doing.

them. But whatever the cause, your dog should stop when the bird gets in the air.

This is chiefly an extension of the "steady-to-wing-and-shot" training. Always "Whoa!" your dog when a bird is in the air, and make sure he stays put until you send him on, or—if you allow him to break shot—until you shoot.

It is okay to shoot over a "stop to flush", should you be within range or should the bird come towards you. Very often, with a bird like ruffed grouse, this is the only shooting you'll get. But in keeping with the axiom that you don't kill birds except when the dog does his job right, *do not* shoot over flushes even though the dog halts, of his own volition or on command, when the birds get up.

## BACKING

Since bird shooting is a sport for sportsmen, "backing" becomes important if you hunt with another dog than your own in the same country at the same time, or if you customarily work a brace of dogs. Otherwise, if only one dog is worked at a time, it's a dead issue.

"Backing" is the honoring of another dog's point. It is an offshoot of pointing, namely sight-pointing, reinforced by a command the dog has learned to obey, "Whoa!" A dog who will not honor another's point,

Training a dog to honor another dog's point: with Orin Benson's "broke" setter already on point, Duffey brings his starting young pointer in from an angle, where she can see both the pointing dog and wind the bird.

Next, the dog in training is brought in from a different angle, so that she *cannot* scent the bird, but will be encouraged to stop and hold a point when she sees another dog on point.

The honoring procedure is repeated from different angles and distances so that the dog will learn to honor another's find, rather than steal the point, or rush past the other dog and flush the birds. The dog is encouraged by stroking and tail-lifting to assume a high, stationary stance when backing, even if game isn't scented.

Here the roles are reversed, and Duffey strokes and steadies his young dog when she makes a find, while Benson brings his setter in to honor the younger dog's point.

but moves in front of the pointing dog to establish his own point, or even worse, flushes the other dog's birds, is a thief. He is a problem; and although it is axiomatic that a dog won't win a field trial by backing another dog's points, more than one dog has lost his bid because of refusal to back. It's not only a pretty sight and a mark of a finished dog, but it's also practical in the hunting field when your partner's dog establishes point and your dog comes in the wrong way on the wind.

The requisite for teaching a dog to back is a second steady, experienced dog, and instant obedience to the "Whoa!" command on your dog's part.

Get the "other" dog set up on point, whether in a natural or planted-bird situation, and then bring your dog into the picture, on check-cord if you aren't sure of his response to the "Whoa!" When he catches sight of the other dog, shout "Whoa!" immediately. Walk to him, stroke him and praise him until your partner has flushed and shot for the other dog. Then cast your dog off again. If there's a doubt in your mind that your dog sees the other one, move him up until he can see, and "Whoa!" him again.

If he doesn't really seem to catch on that he's supposed to "stop and honor" when he sees another dog on point, lead him right up to the pointing dog, where he can pick up the scent. Then when he points (and this will be a point, not a back) pick him up and drop him a couple feet *back* of the pointing dog, and make him hold there until the flushing and shooting are completed.

A dog should learn to "back" on command relatively quickly, since he is actually stopping to the word "Whoa!" just as he did when he forgot his manners and broke. It takes repeated work with another dog pointing to instill the automatic "back on sight" so that your dog will not steal another dog's point, or flush another's birds when both dogs are hunting out of your sight.

The other dog may very well be a "tough cookie" to locate, for he must be steady and positive; let's hope you can find a friend who has an old "broke dog" who's past his prime. If not, you can at least get started on this phase by doing some playing with the bird wing and fish pole, and a second young dog who will also have to be restrained. Obedience to "Whoa!" is the most important element. And, as indicated, if your dog usually will be the only one afield, you can probably forget the whole thing.

## NATURAL RETRIEVING

There are some natural retrievers within the pointing-dog breeds. They are proportionately higher among the Continental pointing breeds

(German Shorthair, German Wirehair, Weimaraner, Brittany Spaniel and Vizsla) than among the pointers and setters. However, the bulk of them must be force-trained to retrieve.

How to start your pointing dog retrieving naturally has been mentioned earlier. Let me emphasize that when I refer to a "natural retriever" I *do not* mean a dog that fetches only when he feels like it. A "natural" retriever, by my definition, is a dog with an instinct or proclivity for picking up and carrying objects in a firm but gentle manner. He is then coaxed or coerced into bringing them to the handler and is praised highly for doing so. While it may seem like a game to him, it isn't. Before he knows what's happening, he's so much in the habit of playing the game according to the rules laid out by the handler that he wouldn't think of doing anything else. He is just as reliable as the force-trained, mechanical retriever, and is much happier and more eager in his execution.

With enough play-training (as outlined in the retriever section) practically any dog can be made into a retriever, by taking advantage of his natural inclinations. However, unless there's a good reason, it makes more sense to stanch a pointing dog before requiring him to fetch. Should you start retrieving first, you are more likely to encounter trouble in stanching your dog.

Play-training to retrieve works better with very young puppies, before they've reached the year to two-year level at which you'd usually turn to such training with most pointing-dog puppies. There are older dogs who can be play-trained to retrieve—not too many, but it's worth a try. Although many dogs within the pointing breeds will readily pick up a dummy or a bird, they often have a tendency to clamp down too hard, or play and chew rather than carry.

So this is the "why" of force-training. It is a tiresome, repetitious, mechanical procedure which inflicts pain on a dog to get him to pick up, carry and release his hold. In effect, he does what he is disinclined to do in order to avoid punishment. There are many force-trained dogs that come to do their work happily. But many also always treat it as just what it is to them, a distasteful chore. For the hunter, however, accomplishing this job is the important thing, regardless of the dog's attitude.

So don't start this work unless you are prepared to finish it. It takes a complete job to turn out a satisfactory retriever.

## FORCED RETRIEVING

Have your dog sit or stand quietly. Take a dummy in your right hand; say, "Dead!" or "Take it!", and open the dog's mouth by grasping his lower jaw, sliding your thumb into his mouth and forcing it open by pressing his lip against his teeth. Immediately slip the dummy into his mouth.

Keep it in his mouth repeating "Hold! Hold!" You may have to hold his jaws closed to keep it there. Sometimes it's quite a tussle, but you must persevere. If he'll hold by himself, a light tap under the chin will keep his head up and his mouth closed on the dummy. Keeping him looking up at you also helps. If he lowers his head, the chances are that he'll drop the dummy.

Then tell him to "Drop!", squeezing his lip against his teeth if he won't release the dummy as you draw it from his mouth.

By backing off a bit at a time and cautioning him "Hold!" it shouldn't take long from the time you've gotten him to accept and release the dummy until he'll sit and hold the dummy while you walk around him. This is done at about the same pace and in much the same manner as the "Sit! Wait!" training procedure.

Then call him to you. If he drops the dummy as he comes toward you, stuff it back in his mouth, tell him to "Hold!" and let him know you are unhappy by speaking harshly. He's got to learn to hang onto the dummy until you say, "Drop!"

Once he'll come to you carrying the dummy, then have him follow you at heel carrying the dummy. Most dogs seem to enjoy this.

Most Pointers must be force-trained to retrieve birds. Here *Dollar* delivers a quail to his owner, Ed Scherer, one of the nation's top skeet shooters.

Now, you must get him to "voluntarily" open his mouth to take the dummy when you say "Dead!" or "Take it!" So you pinch his ear or squeeze a paw. The instant the dog opens his mouth to protest, jam the dummy in it. The sequence is "Take it!"; pinch; insert dummy. The ear pinch doesn't mean you should twist one off—it's just a pinch between the thumbnail and forefinger.

As soon as he has received the dummy, let up on the pinching pressure and tell him to "Hold! Hold!" He should, if he has your previous lesson down pat. To succeed in this kind of work, a dog must master one step at a time. There is no shortcutting. If he doesn't hold, insist that he does or go back and teach him how. You probably won't do this in a lesson or two. But keep at it. Force-training sessions once or twice a day should never run more than ten or fifteen minutes.

After he's learned to take the dummy on command, start to lower the position of the dummy as he takes it toward the floor when you tell him "Take it!" "Dead," or whatever term you're using. You may have to push his head down toward the dummy in your hand until he gets the idea.

The next step is having him pick it up off the floor on command. You may hit a snag here, or it may prove one of the easiest steps. Most dogs that readily accept a dummy from your hand refuse to pick it up from the floor. Others, forced to take it from your hand, go along readily with picking it up. But keep at it.

After your dog is picking up a dummy placed on the floor, drop it in front of him for pick-up. After that, toss it a couple feet from him and order it picked up. He may not want to go out. If necessary, tease him and get him excited about and interested in the dummy before you throw, so he'll *want* to chase and will respond more readily to the "Take it!" Gradually increase the distance of your toss. Remember to praise highly when he does the job, even if it's only half-way satisfactory. To get it completely right, keep working at it.

If your dog goes and picks up, but doesn't want to return with the dummy, start him with a long lead or rope, tossing the dummy just a few feet. When he picks it up, call him to you and pull him in with the lead, repeating until he turns and comes without being pulled. Then work him without the rope.

Once this has been accomplished you've got the problem licked. Now work your dog on retrieving in the same manner as outlined in the chapter on retrieving, the extent of his learning being an optional matter. Plenty of practice and actual field work will keep him sharp. If he balks, go back over the force-training steps.

It makes good sense to first try your dog to see if he has the instincts that conform to my definition of a "natural retriever." Work along natural lines to develop him, if he has. But if he shows no interest or ability, gets stubborn or balky, chews or plays with birds, then move into the force-training method.

There's one last thing I'd better mention: you went to all this trouble because you want your dog to retrieve shot birds. Well, then after he's mastered holding the dummy, you'd best substitute a dead pigeon or game bird and go through the routine again with it before you toss the first bird for him to fetch.

From then on, in retrieving practice alternate the dummies (bare or wing-covered) and dead birds.

# 12

# Training the
# Continental Breeds

Despite their popularity, the Continental pointing breeds (which include German Shorthairs, German Wirehairs, Weimaraners, Vizslas and Brittany Spaniels) seem to be neither fish nor fowl when it comes to finding a book on how to train them.

Instructive tomes on how to train pointing dogs treat the Continentals rather summarily, and no mention is made of them in retriever training instructions. As I write this, I know of no book on the market that is designed specifically to assist the would-be trainer of these general utility pointing dogs.

Perhaps such a book is unnecessary. If you own a dog of one of these breeds, he can be developed into a successful hunter by using, as applicable, the procedures used in training both the pointing dogs and the retrievers, with particular emphasis on the pointing-dog section. Therefore, I ask you to study those sections in this book to glean the training procedures to use with your Continental-style pointing dog.

Although they point their game, the Continentals are different from the pointers and setters which have graced our sporting scene for over a century. But while they are also required to retrieve birds shot over them, they are not in the strict sense retrievers, either. So in a book as ambitious as this, which attempts to show how any gun dog, pointer, spaniel or retriever can be trained, the Continental breeds certainly rate a separate chapter. The better you understand these particular dogs and the proper approach to training them, the better you can apply the basics which have already been outlined in the previous sections on retriever and pointing-dog training.

## PRACTICAL DOGS

The dock-tailed pointing dogs from the European continent are the most practical choice for many hunters who want to shoot over a dog's points, but are baffled or disappointed in the seeming inconsistencies of many pointers or setters. For example, a man who has trained spaniels

One of the "Continental pointing breeds"—*Briar*, a German Wirehaired Pointer—is so intent he almost leans into his birds, as owner Dave Duffey moves in to kick them out and shoot.

and retrievers but now wants to shoot over a pointer will get along better with one of the Continental breeds than with our independent, wide-striding Pointers. Or he may train a Continental or two to bridge the gap before moving into pointing-dog work.

The man who has trained pointers or setters and now acquires a Continental should recognize that some characteristics, which he may consider qualities or defects, are going to be more prevalent among the Continental breeds than among their long-tailed counterparts.

Beyond question, these breeds can be considered practical gun dogs. They can produce for the hunter on any species of upland game bird popular in North America. The fact that they take readily to retrieving, and are much better for limited aquatic work then the pointers or setters, are the major reasons for their rapid rise in popularity since World War II.

But they are not "super dogs," as some overly-ambitious promoters have claimed. They all have to be trained. There is a respectable percentage of duds produced, in common with all other breeds.

Despite their qualities and practical virtues, there are going to be some hunters who simply will not like them. Some guys go for blondes, and so on.

If you have had a setter (Irish, Gordon or grouse-trained English) you'll probably admire the Continentals' method of hunting and work. But if your bird-dog frame of reference is well-bred, ground-gobbling pointers, and setters of the "covey-dog" type, you just won't cotton to most of the Continentals.

For in comparison with the so-called "class" bird dog, most representatives of the Continental breeds appear slow and lethargic, and more inclined to simply "stand" their game than really point it. Even when intensity on point is shown, their neutral colors and docked tails detract from their appearance.

If retriever work has been your delight, the Continentals are not going to display the dash, tenacity, infallible marking ability, serenity under pressure and imperviousness to weather and water that you expect from a good retriever.

Finally, there is the matter of temperament. The "retriever man" is going to think the average Shorthair, Weimaraner or Wirehair is some kind of nut, "a crazy dog." The "Pointer man," who asks little of a dog except that he have insatiable desire to reach out in his search for birds, will decry the Germans' "lack of independence."

The fact of the matter is that the average German dog, possibly in reflection of his dual duties, displays temperament resembling in many ways both pointers and retrievers—which makes up a personality all of its own.

The Brittany Spaniel is another matter. If you've trained retrievers, don't expect that the sensitive and inclined-to-sulk Brit will respond to the rough treatment that a tough retriever shrugs off. If your background has been pointers, by all means encourage the Brit to be as independent as possible. But don't be surprised if he shows as much interest in your whereabouts as he does in seeking game. Unless you are long on patience or can exercise a great deal of self-control, you run the risk of ruining a Brittany who might have become a satisfactory gun dog in another's hands.

To some readers the above will sound discouraging. But it is offered not to discourage, but to point out the possible behavior and reactions you might expect from these breeds (particularly if you've had some experience with others) so that you can gear your training accordingly.

For the fact is that all these Continental breeds are very trainable dogs. Because they respond better to more mechanical yard-breaking and need less field work to be satisfactory as hunting dogs, they are easier for the beginning trainer with limited resources to develop than are most pointers and setters. There's no doubt they're the answer for the man who enjoys keeping visual and verbal contact with his dog in the field and wants his shot birds fetched, but still wants to shoot over a dog's points.

## RETRIEVING

These dogs can be readily trained to retrieve via the "play-training" method outlined in the retriever section, and there's no reason you can't start at the same age you would with a retriever or spaniel pup. You may want to delay the advanced work until after your dog is pointing stanchly.

However, there is less reason to make sure that the Continentals are stanch before seriously working on retrieving than is the case with setters and pointers. Their range is generally restricted, seldom exceeding gun range; thus you can usually get to them faster when they are on point and almost always see them when they hit birds, enabling you to hold them with a well-taught verbal command. They also accept disciplining well if they make mistakes.

If you think retrieving work may or does complicate stanching your dog, you may still be able to continue it by restricting it to water. Your dog will come to associate fetching with water only, and you'll be able to use him on ducks right away. After he's stanch on point, already knowing what the "Fetch!" command means, he can easily be advanced to picking up game on land. What's more, you save a lot of time and also develop a good water worker for the times when upland birds are in and around wet places, or ducks are jump-shot.

Handler Cliff Faestel shows the right motions to make as he asks his German Wirehaired Pointer to sit and deliver.

The retrieving and the introduction to gunfire can be carried out in much the same manner as was outlined in the retriever section. Until almost ice-up time, your Continental breed can be expected to work in water (such as jump-shooting) as long as he keeps moving. However, don't expect him to break ice and then sit quietly in boat or blind. Neither his coat, constitution or disposition is equal to it.

The most is gotten out of the Continental breeds through seemingly contradictory means: firm, no-nonsense discipline, and making a buddy out of your dog.

The Brittany is the exception, for he responds better to "kid-gloved treatment" and patient coaxing while learning, and is not as likely to bounce back without resentment when heavy punishment is meted out for a deliberate transgression. But the Brit, no less than the German breeds, is a poor kennel dog, and much the better for being a companion and family dog.

The German breeds are highly intelligent and seem to be almost begging for training and discipline. They get bored, and often become noisy and destructive if they don't receive enough attention. Finally, they have profound respect and affection for the owner who is Boss— with a capital B.

Because of their heritage—they are used as tracking dogs in Europe— Continentals usually work their game with a lower head and more deliberate manner than the high-headed dash of a good pointer or setter. They like to work foot scent. In the eyes of many pointing-dog *aficionados* this makes "grass-prowlers" out of them, and if overdone, it does. But this tendency to work both foot and body scent can be a moot point. The Continental breeds as a rule are more proficient at recovering crippled game than pointers or setters just for that reason. However, on relocation attempts, the style, dash and positiveness is lacking and may result in taking overly long to produce a hard-running bird.

This can be overcome to a large extent. Don't accept that kind of action from your dog but crowd him and urge him to move on when he starts pottering, accepting your chances of getting either a flush or a "slam-bang, here he is, Boss" kind of point. A dog that handles a running pheasant boldly will have fewer wild flushes than the dog that trails deliberately until the bird tires of running and takes to the air some distance out.

The Continental breeds were meant to hunt close and be under control. In these days of heavy traffic on the highways (and even the byways) and much posting of land and small chunks of game cover, this is advantageous. The Continental may naturally and very profitably work much more on a quartering pattern than on one of long casts. But he should always be busy. Just because a dog isn't a quarter-mile away from the hunter doesn't mean that he isn't hunting and hunting hard.

Bear in mind that just as you may experience difficulty keeping a pointer or setter in close for restricted-cover shooting, you are going to have as much or more trouble getting a Continental dog to reach out in open country. In trips afield always encourage his independence and reaching, for you are much more likely to encounter a dog that won't get out from underfoot than you are to acquire a big-running dog that must be hacked to stay in. These breeds don't possess the desire, physical ability or gait to reach out readily, although at their own pace they can be expected to put in a full day.

Some field trialers have developed individuals and even strains among some of the Continental pointing breeds that might be generously termed "big-running dogs." But they'd never satisfy the requirements of a pointing-dog, field-trial fan on the one hand, while on the other they'd dismay the average hunter who wanted a close-working pointing dog and is happy with a seventy-five to one-hundred-yard range or less.

However, don't ever excuse a dog's hanging around you in the field and general "lack of hunt" by saying, "Well, he's supposed to be a close-working dog." There is nothing more disgusting than a languid, disinterested "shoe-polisher" in the gun-dog breeds.

By the same token, the effort of some real enthusiasts to make the Continental-breed equivalent of a "class field-trial dog" (which even the majority of pointers and setters fail to approach) is just as far off-base. These breeds were not meant to be wide-casting horizon-hunters, for the pleasure of the man who follows his dogs on horseback. They were meant for, gained a following among, and will remain popular with the walking hunter who spends his day trying to find birds to shoot, not looking for his dog.

You will probably discover that acceptable range for a Continental breed will be fifty to one hundred and fifty yards out from the hunter; farther in broken country, but even closer in thick, continuous cover. How far he is from you is of less importance than how ambitiously and intelligently he hunts.

If you haven't already read the sections on the pointing and retrieving breeds but skipped them in order to read about Continentals specifically, please read them now. If you *have* read them, do so again, keeping in mind how you will apply the procedures to your dog; for you can develop him into an eminently practical and useful hunting dog, adaptable to a wide variety of game in any kind of country.

# 13

## Problems and Remedies

The perfect dog doesn't exist. Nor will many of us get a puppy whose development is so smooth that we never have to ask, "What do I do about this?"

You may have read or heard of some dog-training advice that runs along these lines:

"Get a puppy from good breeding, follow this or that procedure, and you won't run into any problems." Since ostensibly there aren't going to be any difficulties with a good puppy and a workable formula, there's no need to mention things that can go wrong, or possible remedies.

I wish I had enough confidence to believe that the "luck of the draw" would furnish you or me with a puppy that would respond to everything we tried to teach him the first—well, at most the second—time we showed him how it's done. You can believe in that possibility if you will, but I'll bet you bump the pot when you're trying to fill an inside straight, too.

Someone once asked me, "How come you so seldom see any training books by professional trainers?"

There could be, of course, a number of reasons, among them the fact that good professional trainers are so darn busy training dogs that they haven't got time to try to put their deeds into words. But that's not the major one.

Having seen, handled, trained, and in some instances failed with so many dogs over the years, a professional becomes a bit leery of making flat statements saying that this or that will work with a dog, period! Since there are so many different approaches and angles to training, a pro must have his doubts about being able to cover everything.

A man who's been lucky in his choice, and has successfully trained one or two good dogs very often has the courage born of ignorance, and will rush in "where old pros fear to tread." If problems arise, the one-dog trainer will tell you confidently, "just get rid of the dog. He wasn't worth starting with anyway." This is a reasonable answer to give if a man has never experienced the problem or attempted to cope with it.

The professional holds his counsel, not because of a reluctance to share knowledge or the hope that he'll make some money on the dog that is a problem, but because he's learned, like any man competent in his craft, that the longer he's around the more chary he should be of making flat statements that apply to all dogs.

Maybe this is all going to sound contradictory, since you've already read my opinion that the dog with "no hunt in him," the overly-shy dog, the spaniel or retriever without fetching instinct and the pointing dog with no pointing instinct aren't worth messing with. But please differentiate between basic lack of talent, and the quirks that you'd like to be able to deal with effectively because the dog possesses other good qualities and is worth salvaging.

Dogs with quirks that can either be remedied or put up with are much more commonly whelped than are "wonder dogs" who just catch on quick. I must admit candidly that I have had, and will continue to have dog problems myself. So have professional trainers, if the "bull sessions" I have carefully listened to are any indication. And every month I try to answer letters from puzzled readers who take their problems to the Dog Editor of OUTDOOR LIFE. So I'm pretty sure you'll have some problems, too, before and after you've trained your dog.

I can't cover all the problems that have come up in developing a field dog, or all the methods that have been used to solve such dilemmas, since my experience isn't that broad and the book isn't that long. I can only tell you of means I have used that worked for me, at least with one dog, and usually with more. Problems around the kennel, barking, chewing, chasing cars and biting the mailman aren't within the scope of this book. Field problems are.

Always bear in mind that what works for most dogs *won't* necessarily work for *every* dog. What works for one dog may not work for others.

Commercial shooting establishments are fine places to train dogs, and here's the author at one of them; he's about to accept delivery of a crippled hen his Labrador has collected.

There's no guaranteed method of success; anyone who tells you that there is, and that putting it magically into effect for ten or fifteen minutes a day will create a trained hunting dog has you pegged as a candidate for the same opium pipe that produces his own fantasies.

So let's get on with. No guarantees, but some solutions that can and do solve problems, and some explanations as to why your dog does things which may lead to your concocting your own remedy.

## HARD MOUTH

"Hard mouth" is a difficult-to-define term. What one man says it is may cause another to disagree. Some would accuse a dog of hard mouth if a dressed bird shows a toothmark, or even if a bunch of feathers adhere to the dog's mouth after he delivers.

Delivery of a bird that's unfit for the table because of the way the

The constant holding and carrying of game and retrieving objects will help to prevent "hard mouth." Here, late in the day, Dave Duffey is still working with a pair of Labs.

dog mouthed it is "proof" of hard mouth—but even this is subject to argument. The fastidious may scream "ruination" because of a tooth-mark, while another will happily gobble down a badly-mashed bird.

Bird mangling must be deliberate and consistent. Inadvertent hard mouth may be caused by a struggling cripple, thick cover or a streak of orneriness or excitement on the dog's part. A dog is *deliberately* hard-mouthed when he crunches down on a bird and rips it up, or runs off and eats it.

Once instilled, hard mouth can be impossible to cure. It's one thing that won't "get better when he gets older." It will get worse. The fact is that many excellent retrievers, as they age, get rough on birds. They aren't hard-mouthed. But through hundreds, yea, thousands of retrieves they've learned that a quick squeeze dispatches cripples and makes everything a bit pleasanter.

The man who says "my dog never ruffles a feather" either hasn't shot many birds over that paragon, or is himself a peerless prevaricator.

In this instance again, prevention is more practical than cure. You shouldn't have problems if you started your pup properly. But they may occur in a really tough dog or in a shy, flighty dog. Because he can be corrected firmly, the job is easier with the tough dog. It's tougher with the sensitive one, who may be working his jaws in excitement and get even more agitated when he's corrected.

If your young dog starts getting rough on birds, utilize part of the force-training method outlined in the pointing-dog section, making him sit and hold a dead bird. If he works it around in his mouth, tap him under the chin until he holds steady, saying "AhAhAh" until he holds it right, and then praise. If he clamps down hard, grab him across the muzzle, pinch his upper lips against his teeth saying "No! No! No!" until he holds it gently.

However, the best preventive as well as corrective measure is fetching and *carrying*, lots of it. Too few dogs are allowed to carry game. They bring it back, the hunter jerks it away and stuffs it in his game bag. This is fun?

In the field, after your dog has delivered praise him, and toss the bird for him again. Or put it in his mouth, order him to heel and let him walk a ways, carrying it. He'll be proud and appreciative as you "talk nice" to him, and when the burden gets a little heavy he'll be eager to turn it over to you.

Around home, put the dog under control and keep something in his mouth constantly, a glove, the mail, a newspaper, sock, dummy or dead bird. Have him carry at heel. Have him sit and hold. When he's this close to you and under control, if he starts rolling the object, biting down or chewing, you can "AhAhAh" him and make him hold firmly but gently. He'll be committing the offense where you can see it and do something about it.

In the field, the damage will be done while he's out of your ken on on the pick-up and return. By the time he delivers, it's too late. So let's hope that your dog isn't incorrigible, and gets the idea that whatever he handles or carries is to be held "just so." Don't give up on a young dog that shows good potential otherwise. He's worth working on, and even fighting with to salvage. If your old dog should go bad, you can try, but you may have to accept it.

Upland game birds, because of their construction and thin skin, are more easily marked and subject to having an intestine squeezed out the anus than are ducks. A dog who's "rough" on upland birds may be a perfectly acceptable waterfowl retriever. But if a dog crunches ducks, or tears their thick hides, you can't say he's rough—he's hard-mouthed.

## WON'T HOLD POINT

Many dogs will lock up on point until a bird moves. When they spot the bird they'll break, and try to catch it. (This occurs frequently with dogs that have been trained to retrieve before being stanched on point.)

To "cure" this, plant birds in trees or bushes. Make a little release-cage out of wire. Put a pigeon in it. Stick the caged bird in the lower limbs of a conifer or in a low bush. Then work your dog past it, where he can get the wind.

He'll home in and point the scent. But although his eyeballs may be rolling, he's unlikely to spot the bird up off the ground. Thus he'll hold long enough for you to reach him—either to talk and handle him, or to get hold of the check-cord, if you think you may have to tip him over. If you can keep him steady with "Whoaaauuup," move up and release the bird (if not, have a helper do it), shooting a blank in the air as the bird flies away. Make the dog hold until you tell him "All right!" If he chases, spill him with the check-cord, stand him in his original place and make him stay. This method can also aid in steadying to wing and shot.

## BLINKING

This is a man-made fault. A "blinker" is a dog who deliberately avoids game he knows is there, or who having established a point, leaves it and moves on pretending to hunt, or comes in to his handler. Some dogs are very crafty about this, and you may discover you have a blinker only when you accidentally "walk up" game. Don't be quick to accuse, however, since some "scenting gremlin" may have goofed your dog. Seek confirmation.

Almost invariably this serious fault is caused by too early disciplining and severe check-cording. The dog comes to associate the punishment with the birds rather than with his misbehavior, so he avoids them. Spaniels and retrievers may also become "blinkers" if the trainer is too early or too zealous in his demands for steadiness.

It will probably cost you a hunting season to correct this unless you can spend a lot of time in the off-season with planted game, encouraging the dog to find birds, and letting him chase. Killing birds over him and letting him fetch will also help. The idea is to have him forget the unpleasantness he's come to associate with birds.

He'll also forget most of his training. So after he gets really "birdy" again, you'll have to start all over—but gently and slowly. The chances are good that with diligent work you'll get him pointing stanchly. But if he's a *really* soft dog you may have to forego steadying, for a while, and perhaps permanently. When you do start stanching and then steadying him, go easy! If he shows signs of being "bugged" again, lay off until his boldness returns.

## LITTLE INTEREST IN BIRDS

Plenty of opportunities and plenty of praise for anything resembling work on birds is all I can suggest here. Some dogs just don't have much "hunt" in them, and there's not much you can do then. Some may lose desire from over-disciplining, or punishment at the wrong time and place. Let the dog chase all he can. Sometimes with pointing dogs it is profitable to develop retrieving as a lot of fun, and to shoot birds at each and every opportunity so that he can get his mouth on them, even if he isn't pointing.

Sure, this is going to compound your difficulties in stanching and steadying. But first things first. If he doesn't hunt, what good is he?

Some quail hunters twist the head off a bird and reward a dog with it. You may want to try it. One famed retriever trainer claims that he assures "birdiness" in his dogs by feeding them the dead pigeons used in training, coping with occasional hard-mouth cases that may arise as a result by using another training procedure.

These actions are based on the theory that a dog hunts because of an atavistic urge to satisfy hunger. So you allow the dog to revert to something we've spent centuries overcoming, to get him to hunt for man and the gun instead of himself. I'm not wild about the idea, but can conceive of using it as a desperation measure. Generally, however, if it's necessary to go this far to make a dog "birdy", lose him.

## LAYS BIRD DOWN, SHAKES HIMSELF

Laying a bird down and shaking upon emerging from water, is a common fault, really not too serious in a hunting dog as long as the dog picks the bird up again and completes delivery without a lot of coaxing. However, it does break the continuity of a nice water retrieve, and is unnecessary.

Don't let it get to be an established habit, or it may develop into the dog's leaving the duck at the water's edge. Besides, you'll cuss every time you flare incoming ducks because you had to do a lot of waving and coaxing to get him to pick it up again.

In training, as soon as the dog approaches shore, start trilling the whistle and running away from him, so that he'll chase you up on the shore. Take the bird on the move if necessary. If he lays it down, get to him fast, tell him "No! No! No!," put the bird in his mouth, make him hold it and then bring it to you. It's a repetitive process. Instill the habit of coming all the way and delivering before shaking off. But always allow a dog a shake before sending him back for more work on multiple retrieves in the water.

## GUNSHYNESS

Your dog won't be gunshy if he was introduced to gunfire properly. But if he wasn't, or some unfortunate occurence (firecrackers, getting shot when running loose) caused fear of gunfire, you have two sensible solutions:

1. Get rid of the dog.
2. Turn him over to a professional.

There are a number of cures; but all take more time than most people are willing or able to spend. They include making a buddy of your dog with gradual introduction to strange noises; the "brave gunfire or don't eat" starvation system; water treatment, with a choice of accepting gunfire or near drowning; or staking a dog out where he can't escape and has to watch other dogs being worked under gunfire.

The starvation method is probably as effective as any and is also the most convenient. Put food in front of the dog and shoot off a cap or a blank. He'll scoot and cower. Remove the food. Don't feed until the next day, when you again shoot as you put the food down. Repeat the next day, and the next, and the next, until the dog gets hungry enough to at least snatch a bite before he runs. Keep at it until he'll gobble his food despite the shot. You may have an emaciated wreck by that time, but the big battle is won—providing he doesn't run away the first time you shoot in the field. If so, it's back to the starvation routine.

## SHYNESS

A shy dog isn't a good prospect to begin with. But you can overcome shyness, if it's not hopelessly bad, by going easier and slower with everything you do, and coaxing and praising rather than punishing. Make sure your dog has complete confidence in you. You can encourage this confidence in many ways, and one way to establish rapport between you and the dog, while you are petting and fussing with him, is by opening his mouth and spitting in it occasionally.

Saliva is one of the first bonds between any dam and her young, through licking and cleaning, so you can often speed up a dog's acceptance of you by expectorating in his mouth. More than one horse has been coaxed and gentled by presenting him with a gob of spit in the palm of the hand when another treat wasn't available. But forget this if you chew tobacco or mints!

## PROFESSIONAL TRAINERS

Pros shouldn't be a problem for you, but your dog may be for them. If you start your dog and then think you can't finish the job, or he comes up with a quirk that you have difficulty coping with, your best friend may be a professional dog trainer. He has facilities and know-how.

This is his livelihood, so you should expect to pay his fee as you would with an attorney or doctor. By the same token, you pay your bill even if you lose the case, an arm or a leg, or the dog doesn't pan out. So first pick a man of good reputation, adequate facilities and clean kennels.

Then give the pro a break. Tell him honestly your dog's faults as well as strong points. Outline what you've done with the dog and the

Professional trainer Orin Benson of Eagle, Wisconsin, shows how to handle a dog on point when you're training for stanchness.

mistakes you made, if you recognize them. It will give him a line on how to treat your dog. If you don't "level" with him, he may make the same mistakes you made and put the final touches on ruining a dog, or at best, he'll have to keep the dog longer and your bill will be higher.

## GETTING BIRDS UP

When a dog is on point, the classic way to approach him is to walk in from behind, and move out ahead and flush the birds. As a practical matter this is done only with a very "well-broke" dog. In training and until your dog is rock-steady, come in from the side or at somewhat of an angle so that the dog can see you approaching. Be brisk and businesslike and don't waste any time, but don't be in a dither.

Pheasants should be trapped between the handler and the dog, in order to assure a flush and a shot.

It is bad form on quail to move in from in front of the dog and flush the birds back over his head. This will greatly tempt him to break and chase. But with pheasant it is a good idea to make a wide semicircle out in front of the dog, and then move in toward him. Pheasants like to run, and with this procedure you can often "trap" a runner between you and the dog, assuring a flush rather than a futile hike behind a dog that must constantly break his points and relocate. With experience, you'll be able to tell from the dog's attitude just about where the bird is in relation to him.

When a dog is sent to "relocate," he is tapped on the head and directed to find birds that have moved on him. Professional Orin Benson shows how with an Irish Setter.

## RELOCATION

It can be argued that once you have cautioned your dog and moved in to do the flushing, he should remain stanch until ordered out to relocate a bird or birds that have left his point. When you can't produce, walk back to your dog, tap his head and say, "All Right!" then cautioning him to "Be Careful, now!" as he moves out.

However, smart hunting dogs will relocate on their own as they learn about birds moving out on them, and this is a highly valued trait—if the dog eventually pins his birds. But if he continually uses a relocation effort as an excuse to flush birds, he should be trained to move out only on command.

If your dog starts to move once you are in front of him trying to produce birds, either "Whoa!" him and continue your efforts, or stand stock still and let him try to relocate on his own. You can't blame the dog for being in motion when the birds get up if you are thrashing around at the same time.

## WHEN IS HE ON POINT

A dog standing in cover, with tail wagging, is usually a puzzled dog. He's got birds, but doesn't know just where. Tell him to be careful if you think it's necessary, but leave him alone and don't walk in until he pin-points the birds and locks up firm. Some dogs never really do firm up. You'll have to learn this about your dog. Most dogs indicate that they are working birds by accelerated tail whip and a break in pace. Others seem to catch their first good whiff of game in mid-stride and come down pointing. It's nothing you can teach a dog.

## SOFTENING ON GAME

Some pointing dogs lose their intense attitude and seem to relax or even cower after they've established point. This is called "softening." If your dog does this you've probably been overzealous in your breaking procedures, and he fears punishment. But some dogs just plain don't give a damn, and show it.

Don't confuse a low-stationed point, or crouch, with softening. It can mean that because of scenting conditions a dog suddenly found himself in the middle of birds and dropped sharply to avoid flushing. Some dogs just naturally point this way at all times. Even if he drops when you approach, it *could* mean he senses birds are about to go and wants to avoid that, rather than a fear of punishment.

But if he loses his rigidity, looks around or even flags (wags his tail), this is softening. Some dogs do this when the birds leave them. Many do it when worked on artificial game (seeming to recognize that this is just another training session, and perhaps associating more discipline and restraint with the planted bird) but are high and hard on wild game.

## FETCHING WOODCOCK

Many otherwise fine retrievers simply won't pick up a woodcock. Why? I've *still* heard no theories that make sense to me. Actually, I think this problem may have been exaggerated, and possibly a lot of dogs that won't pick up woodcock were no great shakes as retrievers in the first place. As a matter of fact, every one of the last twenty-or-so personal dogs I've had all fetched woodcock. It's one of my favorite game birds. But they began carrying them as small pups (see retriever training section) and started in the field with an older dog who *did* fetch them, and got praised for it.

However, this aversion does occur. I've seen a field-trial champion retriever gag when one was finally forced into his mouth, and watched one of my own try to hide a woodcock when she thought she wasn't observed—and then feign ignorance of where it was.

It's not worth making an issue of it. Some dogs seem to develop a certain aversion to certain birds (pigeons being another bird that commonly "bugs" dogs). I had one Lab, soft-mouthed on everything else, who absolutely crunched pigeons. Others had to be forced to pick them up.

# 14

*Stray Shots*

## PICKING A PUPPY

Picking a puppy from a litter is a "by-guess-and-by-gosh" deal, and it's largely a matter of luck. For if you want to get a pup who's young enough to be moulded into what you want, seven to ten weeks is the ideal time; but it's also a time when you can't tell much about your choice.

In practice, however, what your pup turns into will more likely be a result of his environment than any inherent superiority over other pups in the litter. For while any litter may contain a "super dog" or a "palooka", most of the pups will fall somewhere in between. Thus if you're acquiring your dog from a large, impersonally-run commercial kennel that's breeding from established bloodlines, by all means get the pup young. You are assured of his background, and the rest is pretty much up to you.

If you know someone who's raising pups as a hobby rather than as a vocation, you might consider waiting until the pup is four or five months old, which will give you a little more chance to tell about his physical structure and mentality. But do this only when you are assured that the pup gets lots of attention from people and association with places and things, including some play-training. This early association with all the things he's going to live with is most important, and seldom furnished in a large operation where pups are very well cared for as far as feeding, housing and health are concerned, but where they lack casual and frequent contact with humans and life outside the confines of the kennel run.

Take an experienced dog man along with you when you go to pick a pup. He'll be of great assistance, and at least won't let you pick a pup just because he's "cute." For that reason leave the wife and kids at home.

Look for solid, straight bone, clear eyes, good coat and an alert,

Kids and puppies can't get too much of each other. This is the author's son Mike with a litter of Labs.

interested expression. Play with the litter you're picking from and see which ones will chase a thrown glove, or jump up on you demanding attention, or perk up when you clap your hands. These alert, bold ones are the ones you're interested in. But remember, pups are mercurial; the one "sleeping it off" today may be tomorrow's hell-raiser!

Check the pup's mouth to see that his "bite" is proper, neither undershot or greatly overshot. In all sporting breeds, the upper front teeth should close over the lower teeth when the mouth is shut. Also check his navel to see that he isn't ruptured. Unless you are seeking a large or small specimen of the breed, eliminate the giants and runts. Again, this is no guarantee, but it's a pretty good rule of thumb.

Don't consider any pup in dirty, run-down surroundings. But there'll be some excrement and smell around any kennel, so be reasonable. Runny eyes, poor coat, crooked bones or emaciation with a bloated belly indicate a poor standard of care, nutrition, sanitation and parasitic control, making a poor start for a pup, and added vet bills for you.

## PEDIGREE AND REGISTRATION

Nearly every dog has a pedigree, of sorts. So do you. It merely means you know who your ancestors were. Fewer dogs are registered, and seldom will pups be registered individually when you buy them. However, they will usually be *eligible* for individual registration, on the basis of having been registered as part of a litter produced by a registered sire and dam.

The American Kennel Club, 51 Madison Avenue, New York, N.Y. and the Field Dog Stud Book, 222 W. Adams Street, Chicago, Ill. are the two recognized registries for the hunting breeds. You may register in one or both, by filling out, and mailing with the required fee, the application form that is usually provided by the man who sells you the pup. When accepted and certified, this will be your proof that your dog is purebred.

The man who sells you a dog should also be able to show you the pup's pedigree, or those of the sire and dam, although he may or may not furnish you with a copy. The registering agency will furnish you with a pedigree for your dog for a fee. This will allow you to see who your pup's ancestors were and to some extent, what they were.

Unless you've followed canine contests closely, you are unlikely to know any of the dogs listed. But the seller may make a big fuss over a certain famous dog on the chart. If this dog is farther back than grandparent to your pup, don't be too impressed. Some people ask foolishly high prices on the basis of one famed dog that plays a very obscure part in a pup's genealogy. But if the sire and dam, or grandsire and granddam were well-known or titled dogs, pay a bit more attention and be willing to pay a bit more money. If the pedigree of a dog registered with the AKC shows a sprinkling of names preceeded by the letters "F. Ch." or "F. T. Ch.," this is good. This stands for "Field-Trial Champion" and means that the particular dog had the intelligence and ability to learn, and the physical ability to work, and you can hope that his or her descendents have inherited some of these qualities. But if the letters before the name are "Ch.," it means nothing to you as a hunter. This designation means a "Show Champion," a dog judged on appearance rather than ability. Ignore the entry on the pedigree, or if it's pretty solid with show champions, you may even want to avoid buying this pup.

A dog registered with the FDSB is a different matter, since no shows are conducted by this agency, only field trials, with all the emphasis on pointing-dog trials. The AKC licenses or sanctions all retriever and spaniel trials. So when the abbreviation "Ch." (for Champion) appears on the pedigree of a dog registered with the FDSB, it means a trial winner, a working dog. That is what you seek in your hunting dog's background.

## HOT BLOOD

A dog stemming from very excellent field-trial breeding is often referred to as "hot-blooded." Sometimes more emphasis is placed on the "blood" than on the dogs themselves.

Just because a particular dog is an outstanding performer is no guarantee he can transmit his personal qualities to his puppies. Some do, more don't. And some sires who were mill-run in performance turn out outstanding puppies. This ability is known as "prepotency." The same applies to dams, although unfortunately less attention is paid the female than the male line.

Without discounting the importance of "hot blood" and fine selective breeding, you should know that there are a lot of field-trial champion dogs, in all breeds, that you as a hunter wouldn't want as a gift, with a bonus to boot! Most dogs with the fire and drive required to win a championship are too big a handful for the hunter to train, and would give him fits in the hunting field. Just handling such a dog is a full-time job.

Furthermore, once a dog becomes a Champion, the puppies he sires become extremely valuable. So the man who buys one puts it in the hands of the best trainer he can find. No amount of time or money is stinted, and the pups have an unparalleled opportunity to develop properly.

Faults that these pups may possess are often overcome through diligently and ingeniously applied training procedures, and in some cases what the pup may have lacked instinctively has been instilled, by rote and force, by the time he is an adult. So unless a man has seen the dog since puppyhood he never knows whether a field-trial dog's proven ability was based primarily on natural qualities—which can be transmitted hereditarily—or whether he was "hand-made" by an accomplished trainer, thereby displaying talent which has no chance of being transmitted to his offspring.

But let's say you know some fellow hunter who's a farmer, who has a good dog. So has another hunter. Let's say that the two dogs, both of the same breed, both good hunters and of opposite sexes are bred so their owners can "get a pup out of 'em." Neither owner may be any great shakes as a dog trainer—they just hunt a lot. But you've seen their dogs work and you know they're good. What's more, you're pretty sure they are good because of proper instincts rather than proper training, which was probably at a minimum.

There would be some justification in your figuring a pup from this background might turn out as well or better than one with a preponderance of "hot blood" on his pedigree. For if your pup's ancestors were good hunters in spite of, rather than because of their training, you can figure that the chances are good that these natural qualities will be transmitted to a good share of the pups they sire or whelp. For the "cold-bred" dog that doesn't pan out to the satisfaction of his owner is given away or shot, or if he's not smart enough to adjust to a comparatively unsupervised life, he gets himself killed.

It would take some proving, but I'm inclined to bet that if you took two litters of pups, one from hot, field-trial breeding, the other from good-hunting ancestors whose champion forebears are remote or near-nonexistent, and you gave both litters an equal chance with a trainer unapprised of their backgrounds, the pups from each litter who turned into good hunters—or field-trial winners—would be darn near equal.

Sure, blood will tell. I'm not knocking good breeding, which is vital in preserving top-notch field dogs. But prestige, money and reputation will also tell, and this is most often behind the development of outstanding field-trial performers.

I am suggesting that you'll maybe save a row with your wife over money, and still get a good prospect for your needs by doing a little scouting around, locating what might be called a "cold-bred" litter, and making your choice from it. The important thing is that the parents are good hunters and the pups eligible for registration. If there are field-trial champions in the background, wonderful. The more the merrier. But don't let a flock of titles bedazzle you into "betting on the come" and paying four times what you can afford for a pup that you *hope* will be a crackerjack, on the basis of what his ancestors were honed to do perfectly, which you *hope* in turn was founded on natural ability which can be transmitted hereditarily.

## FAIR PRICE

A "fair price" for a dog is what a seller is willing to accept and what a buyer is willing to spend. However, this applies more accurately to trained dogs than to puppies, which are really a big gamble.

It may not win me any friends and probably won't influence any people, but I'll lay it on the line about dog prices and about what you can expect to pay, subject of course to change without notice because of the locality in which you live, the dog's ancestors and the law of supply and demand. (If all those qualifications don't get me off the hook, nothing will!)

First of all, I wouldn't sell an eligible-for-registration pup from any of the hunting breeds for less than $50. I'd rather give them to hunting friends—and I've had to, upon occasion. But you'll have a hard time convincing me that any "pig in a poke", regardless of his pappy's or mammy's accomplishments, is worth more than $150.

You may pay as high as $300, maybe more, for a retriever puppy with a hot field-trial genealogy. But chances are you can find a reasonably well-bred pup for $50. The best Labrador bitch I ever owned was purchased at a farm market at the age of seven weeks for $10. Between $50 and $75 is a fair price, however.

Spaniel prices will about parallel this, with Springers running a bit higher than American Waters or Cockers. (The latter two breeds have little field-trial competition, which produces the automatic "hike" in price that accompanies the title "Champion.")

Much the same can be said about Continental breed prices; they're basically about $50 to $75, but seldom does anyone have the gall to ask more than $150, regardless of breeding. You may pay a bit more for German Wirehairs and Vizslas (on the basis of rarity rather than intrinsic value) as compared to German Shorthairs and Brittanys. Weimaraners bring top prices in some circles, but you can probably locate several at giveaway prices, from some owner who believed all the publicity he read only to discover that he wasn't mining gold, but was competing in a glutted market.

Pointer and setter pups from field-trial and hunting stock are probably the most reasonably priced, although they're somewhat more costly in the North than in the South. Most fanciers and trainers of these breeds are practical dog men, often of rural background; they're familiar with the intricacies and risks involved in animal breeding and husbandry, and aware that money can be used only to develop, not create, natural qualities. You can probably pick up a registerable pointer or setter from hunting stock for $25 to $35. A fair price, again, is $50. Maybe you'll go higher.

While waiting for the next brace of dogs to be put down at an Alabama field trial, a veteran bird-dog trainer mentioned to me that he had a litter of seven puppies, sired by a champion, that would be ready to go soon. I suggested that he shouldn't have too much trouble selling the pups for $150 or more apiece, but that with his considerable talents, he might be money ahead to keep all the pups, break them and then sell at an even better price.

The old trainer's first reaction was a snort. Then he grinned. "Ah s'pose if'n one of yew Yankees wanted to paht with that much money foh a li'l ol' puppy, ah'd be fohced to accomodate yuh. But raht now, Ah got a good-broke dawg foh sale at $250. Put in a lot of tahm on him. So just between yew and me, Ah'd happily sell yuh the whole littuh foh what yew say one pup is w'uth and figuh Ah was money ahaid."

## CARING FOR YOUR DOG

We've all seen dogs that got better care from their owners than most parents give their kids. Yet others are kept in conditions that would make us think they'd be "better off dead." Various people keep their dogs in styles ranging from pampered to impoverished, plus everything in between.

Owning a dog is a responsibility, and it takes some time and effort to care for one properly. Fortunately, however, a dog is one of the healthiest of four-legged creatures, and able to survive with a minimum of care and cost. In some ways, in fact, he's better off when left to his own devices than when pampered, and a pampered dog may well be pitied more than a *slightly* abused one. A fat, spoiled dog isn't comfortable or healthy either physically or mentally, and will never command the respect that's accorded some lean old hound who won't leave a fox or bobcat track until the animal has been shot, holed or treed.

Fortunately too, most dog owners (and let's hope you're among them) charge off the time required to care for their dogs to relaxation and recreation. That's as it should be. Dog care is neither complicated nor difficult, and while some minimum standards must be kept, there are also short cuts which achieve the goal of adequate care without being excessively time-consuming. Few people today are so overworked physically that the activity and sense of accomplishment that comes once the job is done (to say nothing of the dog's grateful reaction to the attention) won't make it all worth the while.

Dog care is really quite uncomplicated and easy, once you know

Concrete kennel runs at the front of the dog house provide adequate exercise space, and keep valuable dogs confined when not being trained.

what you're doing, for the dog requires only six things to stay healthy and happy: a dry, draft-free place to sleep; nourishing food and fresh water; sufficient exercise; some human attention; occasional grooming; and veterinary attention when it's required. A little common sense will go a long way, but if you're a complete neophyte, I'd recommend that you study one of the many excellent books that have been written on the subject of dog care until you've got a firm grasp of the standard practices. No doubt you'll make your own adaptations as time goes on, depending on the needs of your particular dog, your own locality, and the facilities you have available. You'll never go far wrong if you remember to do one thing: *look at the dog* to see how he's doing. His condition, and his expression are the best barometer of the care you're giving him.

A final point that's related both to dog care and to training is the question of where the "dry, draft-free place to sleep" should be located. A lot of people have heard that you can't keep a hunting dog in the house, and that the only place for a bird dog is a kennel outside. But if you want my opinion, there's no good reason at all why the owner of one or two hunting dogs shouldn't have them for family pets as well. In fact, many individual dogs and some breeds in general respond best to this kind of treatment. The more time you spend with a dog and the more tricks you teach him, the better he'll be and the more you can enjoy him. An English Cocker spaniel I owned attended some of my college classes with me, at the express invitation of the professors! A major regret of mine now is that I have too many dogs to have this kind of contact and rapport with all of them. And I'd have to admit that some of the dogs in my kennel right now would be much better for it if they, too, were part of the household.

Be sure, however, that you don't relax your requirement that a dog obey any given command, just because he's around the house and you're only half-paying attention to him. If you tell him to sit or to wait, for example, make sure he does it when he's in the house, just as you'd expect him to if you were concentrating on him in a training session. Too often we tend to be lax with the house dogs, to the detriment of their field work. If you avoid this danger, your dog should only benefit from being a full-time member of your household. And I think you'll find that even though they're not usually advertised as such, the members of the gun-dog breeds rate tops as companions and pets.

## FIELD-TRIAL TRAINING

No book on training hunting dogs should completely ignore the subject of field trials, and this one has no intention of doing so. For if you like dog work, nothing beats a field trial except hunting.

This statement will, I hope, keep things in their proper perspective. Yet there are many sportsmen who seldom if ever hunt, but who own dogs that run in field trials or handle them in trials themselves. Something like fifty to sixty thousand dogs compete in various field trials for spaniels, pointing dogs and retrievers each year.

Most books about hunting-dog training are written for field trialers by field trialers, and if it's field trials that you're interested in, I'm afraid you're in the wrong pew. I've tried to aim this book at the hunter, because I'm primarily a hunter myself. As far as dogs are concerned, it's hunting that's my "meat and potatoes"; field trials are just the gravy. So it seemed a waste of time for me to write a book detailing field-trial procedures and training methods. The man who's already involved in

The German pointing breeds are required to fetch as well as point; here's a German Wirehaired Pointer making a delivery to her handler during a field trial.

trials probably knows as much as, or more than, I do about training; a rank beginner wouldn't understand all the details anyway; and the man who is primarily interested in training hunting dogs wouldn't benefit greatly from trial training procedure.

Nevertheless, any man with a hunting dog should understand something about trials and take in as many as he can, just to see how proficiently a dog *can* be trained. And above all, he should refrain from "knocking" trials as some kind of fancy show that doesn't have anything to do with hunting dogs. (At the same time, the field-trial fan should button his lip about the "hunting tests" that judges give, and the idea that "trials are *just like* hunting, except that the dogs have to be better", etc.)

For—let's face it—field trials are *not* hunting. In some ways they can simulate it, but they can never duplicate it. Field trials are a highly competitive game, bearing about the same relationship to actual hunting that trap and skeet shooting do to actual field-shooting on game birds. So people who favor field trials need make no apologies for their sport, nor do they need to justify its existence.

In fact, two things should be pointed out. Field-trial enthusiasts have done more for the general improvement of our bird-hunting dog breeds than any other group in the dog world, from the standpoint of producing dogs that are valuable to the hunter. Due to today's lack of game and extensive hunting restrictions, the place to really prove a dog—granting the artificialities that surround it—is a field trial. (This is not to say that control of hunting-dog production is not without its dangers, for in some instances, "made" dogs rather than "natural" dogs are perpetuating the breed, and this can only be to the general detriment.)

Secondly, if men are going to prize really good dogs and get a full measure of enjoyment from them in the future, field trials will probably be the answer. For trials can be conducted either without actually killing game, or with the use of domestically-raised birds, and thus they cause no depletion of the stock of natural game. In fact, field trials are extremely beneficial to conservation activities. Not only do they assure trained dogs in the field and thus reduce the waste of shot birds which are lost by dogless hunters, but field trialers are also usually in the forefront of efforts to preserve game and its habitat in their natural state, for the enjoyment of both the dog fanciers and the general public.

It's also wise to recognize that you, as a hunter, will seldom be satisfied with a dog of field-trial caliber and field-trial training. Whether it's a spaniel, a retriever or a pointing dog, the top trial dog will be just too much dog for you. Because of the time and intensive training that go into developing them, many trial dogs are far from being well-balanced, well-adjusted dogs. Through a combination of their breeding and their intensive, selective training, many of these dogs are little more than superlative competitive machines, comparable to Thoroughbred race horses. Sure, a fair number of trial dogs are capable of becoming fine hunting dogs, given the proper training and exposure; and fortunately, there are some very precious dogs who can, and do, both hunt and compete in trials. But in general, the people who contend that there's no difference in the approach to training a field-trial and a hunting dog haven't really thought it out.

Don't get the idea that you can't get a lot of fun out of field trials if you go in the right frame of mind. And competing in field trials will give your dog experience and keep him conditioned the year 'round. It will also force you to train your dog better, for even if you don't expect to win, you won't want to put down a dog who might shame you. What's more, you'll meet a pile of fine, interesting, highly competitive people who are interested in the same thing you are—dogs, and dog work.

For information about the "when and where" of bird-dog trials, write to The American Field Magazine, 222 West Adams St., Chicago, Illinois; The American Kennel Club, 51 Madison Ave., New York, N.Y.; or Miss Leslie Anderson, Secretary, Amateur Field Trial Clubs of America, Hernando, Mississippi. If it's retrievers or spaniels you're interested in, contact The Retriever Field Trial News, Grange Bldg., 435 East Lincoln Ave., Milwaukee, Wisconsin, or The Springer Bark, San Leandro, Calif.


Don't expect to make a big splash when you jump into this game. It takes a lot of time and money to develop a top field-trial performer, and men have spent literally tens of thousands of dollars before coming up with a Champion. Amateur stakes and trials for amateur handlers are available, but bear in mind that the only thing "amateur" about the stake is the handler himself; most of the dogs will have had extensive work with professional handlers. So wade in gradually by watching some trials first, and then trying your dog in some of the "small-time" local trials, or just "fun" trials put on by a dog or gun club.

Then if you're really bitten by the "field-trial bug", be prepared to wind up right up to your hips in dogs. For if you visualize fame and perhaps even fortune, you'll have to go through quite a few dogs before achieving it, unless the lightning stroke comes as a lucky break. If you take up this sport for recreation it may be that you can have a "fun" field-trial dog and a good hunting dog in the same animal. But if you're going to take the sport seriously (or have to win to satisfy your ego), but still continue to enjoy hunting—then you'd better figure on owning at least two dogs, one for trials, and one for hunting.


## TRAINING HELP

Lacking help in the form of an interested wife or children, by all means try to get a friend or neighbor interested in hunting dog activity too. Some aspects of training just aren't done easily alone. Two dog men can help each other, one acting as bird thrower or doing the shooting while the other concentrates on his dog. The cost of pigeons, game birds, equipment or the training and hunting trips can also be shared. Joining a club or training group may also be worthwhile if you can avoid the politics and petty jealousies that so often beset dog organizations.

## KEEPING IN TOUCH

Some dogs, while hunting hard, seldom lose track of the men they are hunting with. They keep in touch. This is a highly desirable quality in a gun dog and the best of field trial pointing dogs have it, showing to the front at frequent intervals and heeding the voices of their handlers to make the turns in a course. All hunters want their dogs to stay with them and hunt for them, but too many are cursed with virtual runaway dogs.

How does a man assure himself of a dog he can depend upon not to be gone for extended absences, a dog that will hunt in the general direction the man has chosen, checking in occasionally or seeking out the hunter if exigencies or accident cause them to lose each other for a time?

While there is something that can be said for the dog's "natural bent", some dogs being simply more independent or wild than others, for the most part the responsibility for and the joy in having a gun dog as interested in keeping in touch with you as you are in keeping track of him lies with you, the trainer.

You can accomplish this in a very simple way that will be good for both of you. From the time you get your puppy take him (or the whole litter, if you have more than one) walking in the field. Walk, walk, walk. Encourage his independence as he gets older and bolder but insist that he be with you constantly.

Never let him run loose, unsupervised and without you. If from toddling puppyhood on you are always with your dog when he is taken afield you become an integral part of the game. You're always there. He develops the habit of looking to you for a cue, heeding the direction you take and expecting your praise and punishment. When done often enough and starting at an early age your presence on the hunting scene will become so much a part of your dog's life that it becomes inconceivable to him that he can be out there on his own.

Runaway dogs, as is the case with most faults, are man-made, not born. Turn out a year-old dog who has hardly been out of the kennel and seldom taken afield and you are virtually sure to have control problems, with the solution at best difficult and at worst impossible. It's not enough to fuss with him in the house and around the yard. You must go afield with him too. The earlier and oftener, the better. Using your head and your legs from the pup's weaning time until his first opening day will save your lungs, heart and disposition and make you the envy of every gun dog owner who goes afield a stranger to his dog. Walk your puppies, gentlemen!

## YOU'D BETTER BELIEVE IT

Just as your dog must trust you, so must you trust your dog. If a pointing dog disappears, head for the direction you last saw him. Maybe he won't be on point. But on the chance that he is, you'd better get there, even if it means busting brush or wading creeks.

If your spaniel or retriever shows by his animation that he's "making game," move up close, fast. If you don't honor a dog's finds he may conclude you just aren't interested. That's why a gun dog doesn't work meadow larks and other "stink birds" whose scents could be attractive. You have shown no interest in shooting them. So stay with him if he's a flush dog, find him if he's a pointer.

Do I practice what I preach? Usually. But a couple times a year I bend over and let a hunting buddy plant a boot mark on the seat of my pants . . . because I didn't trust my dog. While hunting quail in southern Illinois with Art Reid, outdoors editor of the Carbondale, Ill. newspaper, a young Pointer bitch being trained got out of sight. I stood for two or three minutes, whistling and calling, only to be startled by the rise of a huge covey from a woodlot, 60 yards to my right. And there stood the little bitch, high and hard, probably wondering, "What in heck does that guy want from a lady?"

I sat down rather gingerly all evening. Reid is a tall man with long legs and big feet. He packs quite a wallop.

## HANDLING

Too few dogs are handled. Too many are shouted, whistled and waved at incessantly by men who *think* they are handling. Whistles, shouts and waves should mean something. Carry on a steady stream of blather and the dog will react in two ways: he'll either ignore commands or depend upon them. Neither is good.

Nothing spooks game more than a human voice. A good-handling dog requires a minimum of noise, but obeys when a shout or whistle is necessary. So don't go on hacking a dog. Save your breath for times when your dog really has a bawling out coming.

## STARTING A PUP WITH AN OLDER DOG

Giving your pup a start in the field with an older trained dog is a good idea, if another dog is available. An experienced dog will show a pup a lot and find some game for him. But don't overdo it. It can make the pup dependent on the old dog and can have a deleterious affect on the already trained dog. More than one young dog has never developed or, at best, became a lackadaisical hunter because he came to depend on the more experienced dog to produce game . . . or got discouraged when he couldn't keep up. And more than one trained dog has defied his master and deliberately fouled up because he was disgusted with a blundering pup or jealous of the attention the pup received or the things he was allowed to get away with.

Along the same lines, should you have a pair of dogs and one is clearly superior to the other, while competition will often fire up an otherwise indifferent dog, the superior and inferior dogs should be hunted together only occasionally. No one, man or dog, can stand up under being a permanent loser.

## TEMPTATIONS

Don't keep your young dog in some kind of a vacuum and then get shook up when some unknown temptation provokes misbehavior. If you'll be hunting in farming country, expose him to chickens, cattle, sheep and other livestock. If he wants to chase, you can call him off larger livestock and punish him quite severely.

Should livestock spook your dog, give him confidence by walking around and through barnyards and pastured herds at heel or on leash. Walk him through a yard or penful of chickens on leash and reef him good if he indicates even an interest in domestic fowl. Don't worry that it will bother his hunting on wild game. Dogs raised and trained on game farms learn to ignore penned pheasant and quail but hunt them avidly once they are in the field.

Expose him to everything he's likely to encounter in daily living, encouraging him if he's frightened, scolding if he's aggressive. Teach him that some things simply must be accepted or even ignored.

## PEN-RAISED GAME BIRDS

Artificially propagated game birds play an important part in the training of a gun dog. For most sportsmen and trainers they are all that's available. But keep a couple of things in mind.

Pheasants released only a few hours before you hunt them or train on them pose no serious problems in the training of a gun dog. Quail do. A gun dog can have all his training on hand-reared pheasant and acquit himself very well on native birds. But unless the released quail have been out for weeks at a time (as they may be on really well-run shooting preserves) your dog will find that hunting wild quail is a whole new ball game.

Recently planted quail tend to sit too tight, thus a dog will get careless about pointing them and inadvertently flush wild, shot-over coveys that won't tolerate a "right under the nose" approach.

Recently released quail also tend to "straggle out" when flushed, rather than roar up in a single covey flush as wild birds are expected to do, as well as run on the ground, or individuals will fly weakly.

This can be disastrous with a youngster, who naturally will chase the flushed birds. If he doesn't catch a weak flyer, when you call him back to the area of the flush to work on your stanching techniques, chances are good he will find, dive in and catch a tight-sitter or runner. If catching birds becomes ingrained, you will have one helluva job stanching a pup.

Use recently planted quail chiefly when you are going through the mechanical procedures of teaching stanchness and steadiness to wing and shot . . . when the pupil is on a check cord. Shoot on preserves that random release their birds rather than stock before the gun. Then give your dog all the experience possible on native birds. He won't have earned the title or the respect accorded a good bird dog until he learns the difference and can handle the natives.

## CHANGE IN SCENERY

When taking your dog afield, expose him to as much different country as possible. If you train in the same place each time he may have trouble adjusting to something new. If you are trying to develop a dog for use in ruffed grouse and woodcock cover it's foolishness to use a cow pasture for his workouts. Put him down in the country and cover in which you expect him to work most often. Then he'll learn how to handle himself.

If you do make a big switch, like going from a northeastern grouse covert to southwestern quail venues, be tolerant of your dogs' inability to produce like the native dogs do for a day or two until your dog adjusts and can spell out the name of the game.

## RIDING IN THE CAR

Getting "car broke" is a must for today's dog. Seldom will he reach the hunting grounds in any other way. He'll come to love it when he connects car rides with getting out in the field. After he has learned to sit and stay and is accustomed to the car, make him stay in one place on the floor or seat so he'll get used to being quiet rather than ramming about.

If you hunt often or make long trips, invest in a wire car crate. This will be his "home away from home" and the practical conveniences of using these travel crates are too numerous to mention, at home and in motels, as well as on the road.

You'll save yourself a lot of problems, including car-sickness, if you start taking a tiny pup along in the car with someone holding him for short rides of two or three miles at first and gradually lengthening the trips. Frightened dogs thrown into a car and not being accustomed to it, or reassured, are more susceptible to motion sickness. Then up-chucking can become a reaction rather than a real malady. If you have a dog that gets car sick you may be pleasantly surprised to find that if you position his travel crate so he is riding cross-wise, rather than facing front or back, it will reduce or eliminate this nuisance.

## STICKS AND STONES . . . AND BALLS

Don't allow playing with your dog in the form of throwing a stick or ball for him to fetch. If you've taught him properly at an early age he should recognize that a dummy or bird is the thing he's to pick up and carry . . . properly.

Caution the kids about this. If they throw a ball, stick or stone and finally let the pup run off and chew it, or chase him around the yard, he'll try to play this game with a dummy or bird. Kids tossing sticks into the water, picking them up again when the dog gets them and drops them on shore and throwing them out again is in the same category.

I've cured dogs of this habit of laying everything down on the shoreline, then had the owner-family show up to "see how our dog is coming along," and had the dog revert to his old habits in their presence, a matter of association. Sure, some dogs are discerning enough to know the difference between work and play. But don't count on it, least of all with a young dog in training.

## KIDS AND DOGS

Don't let's get the idea from the above that I'm saying kids and dogs don't mix. They're the greatest thing that ever happened to each other from the time of cuddly puppyhood until stiff-jointed retirement. Nothing helps more in developing a well-adjusted, easy to train dog personality than letting the canine tag along with the kids.

Kids and dogs have an affinity for each other. A youngster will accidentally introduce a dog to a lot of stuff you'd have to work at thinking about, accustoming him to things through play that are difficult to do formally. Nor are children reluctant to carry on conversations with animals, and talking to a dog *is important*.

But make sure they understand that if they use any of the commands you've taught the dog they must see that they are obeyed. Nor should they be permitted to conduct training sessions unless you can supervise; but kids are a great help in shooting guns, throwing birds and doing the legwork training sessions require.

They'll quickly pick up what to do and what not to do from your example and from the time they're 10 years old may be entrusted to do some training and brushing up work for you. Better yet, get your sons or daughters dogs of their own to train and you can work together. It's surprising how good a job an interested pre-teenager can do.

But alas, about the time they get really proficient, they'll discover the charms of the opposite sex and dogs will become dull and boring. Yet, the work they do with dogs as children may serve them well when they regain their perspective.

## ANTICIPATION

As you gain experience with your dog or dogs, you'll be able to anticipate what a dog is likely to do and when. Stop him before he does it, if it's wrong, or encourage him if he slacks off something he should do right. When you've developed this knack, it's much easier to head off something than to correct an act already committed.

❀    ❀    ❀

There, now you've got a start. More than a start, in fact; for you've got an insight into how to go about acquiring and developing the finest hunting companion a man can have—a dog that suits the game he's hunting, knows his job, and suits *you*. As you've seen, it really doesn't take much more than a little careful thought, a little common sense, and a little time. But I hope my words may have helped you to avoid some false starts and wasted efforts, and to speed down the same pleasant path that has so greatly enhanced my own hunting enjoyment.

Good luck, and good gunning!

# Index